Supporting Local Businesses and Entrepreneurs in the Digital Age

Supporting Local Businesses and Entrepreneurs in the Digital Age

The Public Librarian's Toolkit

Salvatore DiVincenzo
and Elizabeth Malafi

LIBRARIES
UNLIMITED™

An Imprint of ABC-CLIO, LLC

Santa Barbara, California • Denver, Colorado

Library of Congress Cataloging-in-Publication Data

Names: DiVincenzo, Salvatore, author. | Malafi, Elizabeth, author.
Title: Supporting local businesses and entrepreneurs in the digital age : the
    public librarian's toolkit / Salvatore DiVincenzo and Elizabeth Malafi.
Description: Santa Barbara, California : Libraries Unlimited, an imprint of
    ABC-CLIO, LLC, [2017] | Includes bibliographical references and index.
Identifiers: LCCN 2017018087 (print) | LCCN 2017034235 (ebook) | ISBN
    9781440851520 (paperback) | ISBN 9781440851537 (ebook)
Subjects: LCSH: Libraries and business—United States. | Libraries and
    business—United States—Case studies. | Business—Computer network
    resources. | Business—Bibliography.
Classification: LCC Z711.75 .D58 2017 (print) | LCC Z711.75 (ebook) |
    DDC 021.2—dc23
LC record available at https://lccn.loc.gov/2017018087

ISBN: 978-1-4408-5152-0
EISBN: 978-1-4408-5153-7

21 20 19 18 17   1 2 3 4 5

This book is also available as an eBook.

Libraries Unlimited
An Imprint of ABC-CLIO, LLC

ABC-CLIO, LLC
130 Cremona Drive, P.O. Box 1911
Santa Barbara, California 93116-1911
www.abc-clio.com

This book is printed on acid-free paper ∞

Manufactured in the United States of America

Contents

Preface   vii
Acknowledgments   xi
Introduction   xiii

CHAPTER 1: The Business Librarian   1

CHAPTER 2: Setting Up Your Space   15

CHAPTER 3: At Your Service   23

CHAPTER 4: Deep in the Data   33

CHAPTER 5: Some of the Best Things in Life...   49

CHAPTER 6: Old School: A Quick Note on Print   59

CHAPTER 7: Programming and Special Events   65

CHAPTER 8: Reaching Out Is (Not) Hard to Do   87

CHAPTER 9: Stories from the Front Line   97

Conclusion: Did You Get All That?   107
Bibliography   109
Index   113

Preface

The Who, What, and Why

We know what you are thinking: who the heck are these two and why are they writing a book about business librarianship? Here are our stories.

Salvatore

I never had an intention of becoming a librarian, by any stretch of the imagination. Quite frankly, doing what I do now, 10 years in, is still somewhat alien to me. It's also the first time that I've been focused in what I do career-wise. Like most high school students growing up on Long Island, when I was 16, I got a job as "maintenance associate" at Leewards (now known as the retail craft mega chain Michael's). It wasn't difficult work—sweeping glitter and errant glue sticks from the floor, stocking out bushels of eucalyptus leaves, and my favorite: planograms. Perhaps this was my first foray into the world of librarianship, or rather, organizing things like a librarian would. We'd get a picture of how the shelf should look, along with a box of labels, all the hardware, and boxes of merchandise to fill each spot. There was something incredibly satisfying for me to start off with a blank six-foot section of aisle space and transform it into something sellable.

As my time at Leewards progressed, I moved from cashier, to senior cashier, to custom picture framer, to frame shop manager. This was my first foray into management and business. I supervised four picture framers and had to work on schedules, budgeting, ordering, and so on. While the frame shop was part of the overall retail operation of the store, it was very much treated as its own entity, one of the reasons being we had big, single sale transactions compared to the rest of the store. (The average transaction was usually over $100.) This gave me a little more flexibility in what I did in the shop in terms of marketing, organizing the workflow, and training. In many ways, it was like running my own business.

After a couple of years, I felt the itch of moving on to something more challenging. So I jumped at the chance of working for an interactive marketing firm in the heart of New York City. *Complete and utter culture shock.* Going from my relatively sleepy-town neighborhood's retail operation to commuting two hours a day to the hustle and bustle of midtown Manhattan and, for me, working with high-energy professionals was an incredible experience. My supervisor lived in a mansion; he had dinner plans with the heads of record labels and television channels. Suits and ties. Lunch meetings. I learned what the term "corporate culture" meant.

Before I knew it, I was courted by one of the department heads to leave with her and go to another company, this time downtown. Another corporate culture, this time more like you hear they have at Google and Facebook. *Free pizza every Friday afternoon and unlimited soft drinks all day!* There was no such thing as "casual Fridays" there; it was casual everyday: jeans and t-shirts. Regardless of the look and feel of the place, I sat in meetings with executives from Coca-Cola, John Deere, and Gateway Computers.

At the same time, I started my own consulting and website design business. One of my clients turned out to be my local library. I ended up redesigning their website as well as doing some adult and teen programming. It was my first experience working in a library, and it eventually ended up being my "in."

The commute was too much for me. I had spent most of my day on a train and most of my nights worrying about catching the aforementioned train the next day. I escaped New York City and found a job at a very small, family-owned software company close to home. There I was able to see another side of business, the one that I now deal with regularly: people with great ideas but not a huge amount of money. We did our best to grow, and I was able to scale some of my New York City experiences to this company. The company ended up moving to Arizona, and I went with them. Unfortunately, their New York success did not translate to Arizona success. One day my boss gave me some money for groceries and said he hoped to get me my paycheck soon. Unable to guarantee a regular paycheck every week, I returned to home to New York where I could live rent free for a while without a job. I was out of work for six months, constantly interviewing and searching for something, experiencing unemployment for the first time. I was living the "talent transition" life, and looking back at it now, it was an experience that I still relate to today when a patron who is looking for a job comes in to use our services.

Finally good luck came to me, and I was pursued by a former colleague for a position in retail management, which I gladly accepted. While it was fantastic to be working again, it wasn't exactly what I wanted to do with the rest of my life; but it was a great experience nonetheless. I was able to build my customer service skills, use my marketing background to come up with promotional materials, and use my technical background to streamline our in-store order-taking process. Just when I was ready to consider moving on to something else, another change came: after three years, the corporate office was closing my location. Not wanting to let me go, I was moved to a sales position for the company at their corporate office. Again, another angle in the business world: this time I was cold calling clients and perfecting my sales pitch. It wasn't quite my cup of tea. Frankly, it was torturous. I was uncomfortable with what I was doing every day. I wanted out, and I had to get out and find not a job, but a career. When the assistant director of the library I had been consulting for mentioned in passing that I should think about becoming a librarian, I took it as a sign. That was 10 years ago.

The point to this long-winded dash down memory lane is that all these experiences help me every day. I'm able to guide patrons down paths not just from my experience as a business librarian but from my experience in the small business world, the home-based business world, and the corporate world. Is it necessary to be a successful business librarian? *Absolutely not.* Is it helpful? You bet.

It was a natural fit for me to be placed in my department at the Miller Business Center. To be frank, when I finally became a librarian, I thought that my days of the sales pitch, business networking, and meetings with big companies were over. *Boy was I wrong.* For all intents and purposes, I'm still in business.

Elizabeth

I'm that annoying person who picked a career because I love books. *No, not librarianship*—publishing. After two years of community college, I was looking for a major. I loved books and literature but thought my only options were to be a teacher or a writer. I found out that a local college had an English major with a concentration in Publishing. It clicked for me. It felt right and it was. I loved learning about the industry from experts, and I was convinced I would be the next great editor and have my own imprint by the time I was 30.

HA! An editor came to speak at one of my classes during my last year and pegged us all. She said, "I know you all want to be editors, but editorial assistant jobs are few and far between. Take whatever publishing job you can get as you are more likely to be hired in editorial from within." I did just that, accepting an assistant position in the Special Markets department at what was then called PenguinUSA (now a part of Penguin Random House). In publishing, Special Markets departments are responsible for sales to nontraditional venues such as gift shops, department stores, and mail order catalogs. It wasn't exactly my dream job, but I ended up loving the challenge of it. I spent a lot of time matching books with different outlets and making my sales pitch. I got to travel around the country with sales reps to meet with different clients—everyone from the owner of a small gift store to the merchandise buyer at the Metropolitan Museum of Art. I quickly realized that this is where I fit and forgot about moving over to editorial.

After a couple of years at PenguinUSA, I went to Scholastic Entertainment, a quickly expanding division of Scholastic Inc. encompassing Special Markets, movie, and television production and licensing. This is where I really grew. In addition to managing a commission sales force of more than 75 reps, I coordinated our attendance at several major shows and worked with our biggest accounts. I also handled more custom deals that included special printings, which entailed matching the perfect book with the perfect client. Sounds a little like reader's advisory, right?

Eventually I left Scholastic for Facts On File, which gave me an opportunity to work with a less commercial publisher and get my first introduction to the library publishing industry. One of my early responsibilities was Subsidiary Rights, which was way out of my comfort zone but gave me the opportunity to go to Frankfurt Book Fair and negotiate with foreign publishers.

While I really enjoyed my job, in the back of my mind I was always thinking about what my next step would be. I decided to begin the process of getting an MLS by taking one class a semester over five years. I thought I would get my degree and then "retire" to a quiet job in a library when I was 40. *Are you laughing as you read that sentence?* I laugh at myself when I think about it now.

In hindsight, I realize that I knew close to nothing about actually being a librarian. I was so fortunate to have had a teacher who became my mentor: Luise Weiss really guided me toward a career in public librarianship. When I was approaching graduation, Luise began talking to me about the business services at Middle Country Public Library—services that would soon become the Miller Business Center. Suddenly it all clicked for me. I could be a librarian and a businessperson. When the offer came in to work at the only business center on Long Island, I jumped at the chance. I had little practical experience in general or business librarianship, but I knew I would have a lot of support.

And I did. The knowledge I brought with me from my corporate career was invaluable, but I still relied heavily on my colleagues and peers. I threw myself into business librarianship and haven't looked back. More than 10 years later, I know a lot more, but I am still learning.

We've been in the trenches. We know what it's like in the business world. It's not easy. Perhaps you too have been there before in some capacity. It is not necessary to have come from the corporate world or a small business, to be a good business library. Will it help? Sure. Empathizing with your patrons will add a little extra to what you do, but it won't make or break you. While our paths were not direct, they landed us here and we're happy they did.

Remember This

There is no cookie-cutter business librarian. Our unique experiences and skills give businesses and entrepreneurs a more vibrant experience.

Acknowledgments

Thank you to librarians who gave us their time and insight into business librarianship. Many of their stories are included in this book.

Thank you to our colleagues at the Middle Country Public Library, especially the Miller Center team, who encourage and inspire us every day.

And a big thanks to our families and friends who gave us unconditional support during the writing of this book.

Sal would like to thank Elizabeth for being as cool as a cucumber during this process.

Elizabeth would like to thank Sal for lighting the fire when needed.

Introduction

Changing Role of Libraries

The stories are everywhere. People have Google, Netflix, and Amazon; why do they need libraries? Only people who have never been in a library can possibly think that we don't need libraries. Libraries have always been trusted institutions focusing on lifelong learning. While the methods in which the teaching is delivered may change, libraries will continue to adapt and offer these opportunities.

Why It Is Important for Libraries to Help the Business Community

Sari Feldman says, "Libraries are kind of support systems and community networks at different life transitions" (Dalton 2016). Those transitions include career changes and entrepreneurial endeavors. Never was this truer than during the 2008 economic collapse. People turned to libraries. The unemployed came to the library in droves to use computers and printers, for help in writing a resume and cover letter, to prepare for upcoming interviews, and to investigate the possibility of becoming an entrepreneur, a small business owner. Now, almost 10 years later, we are still seeing entrepreneurs and business owners working 24/7 to keep their businesses strong. The importance of the services you can provide a business is greater than ever.

Small businesses are the economic engine of our country. According to the Small Business Administration, small business is big and accounts for 54 percent of all U.S. sales. And since the 1970s, small businesses have provided 55 percent of all jobs and 66 percent of all new net jobs (SBA 2016). Small business is crucial to the economic success of our country and of our region. We know that economic prosperity for the region can translate into success for library with funding through taxes, donations, grants, jobs, and increased library support from patrons.

Librarians should think of the business community as another patron base. We target senior citizens, children, teens, and new adults with specialized programming and resources. These groups then talk about your library and increase awareness throughout the area. The business community is no different. They will spread the word about your services. If an entrepreneur sees value in the services you offer, he or she will tell other people.

Librarians and entrepreneurs are kindred spirits. Libraries often do more with less and sometimes face challenge to continue offering some services to our patrons. We appreciate the struggle to find what is needed to succeed and understand how vital it is for success. It's not just about the resources; it is about the guidance and support they receive from the library.

Why This Book Is Needed

More and more libraries are seeing an increased need to offer business services or expand the services they are currently offering. From our experience we know that many librarians are being thrown into business services without much support. Although more and more libraries are starting up business centers and offering programs and services to businesses, it is still not as ubiquitous as it should be.

You may feel like an outsider in your organization. Not everyone will get it. To some librarians, business services sound b-o-r-i-n-g. We are here to tell you it is not. Sure, on the surface, a program on the intricacies of worker's compensation for the self-employed doesn't sound as exciting as say, that tie-dye t-shirt program being offered in the children's department, but believe us when we tell you that there is nothing better than hearing stories from entrepreneurs who are growing and succeeding and supporting themselves with their endeavors.

Survey Says

When we were first approached to write this book, we thought we would survey business librarians to get some ideas on what they are offering their business patrons. We sent out an invitation via social networking, listservs, and simply word of mouth. Of the over 100 librarians who graciously responded, 51 percent were academic librarians (Figure I.1). For us this was very telling and not surprising. While this is changing, many public librarians consider themselves librarians, even if they have a specialty or end up working with a particular group almost exclusively. They may be the point person for entrepreneurs at their local library, but they still would not call themselves a "business librarian." We understand the hesitation to call yourself a specialist, but we urge you to remember that librarians are specialists in guiding people to the information. You can guide people to the information they need on a specific mutual fund without a degree in finance.

The other most telling result of the survey was the level of experience of the respondents, among whom 42.3 percent are new to business services within the past five years. Thankfully, 33.7 percent have more than 10 years' experience (See Figure I.2). We are here to help!

How This Book Can Help Get You Started

Both authors came to librarianship as a second career, and neither expected to become business librarians. While we were fortunate enough to have a very supportive administration and experienced colleagues to guide us, our experience shows us that many librarians making their first forays into business reference are not as lucky we were. Our goal with this book is to give you a

Librarian Type

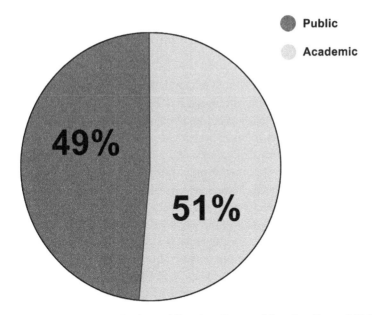

Figure I.1 Great Big Business Librarian Survey: Librarian Type, 2016

Number of Years in the Profession

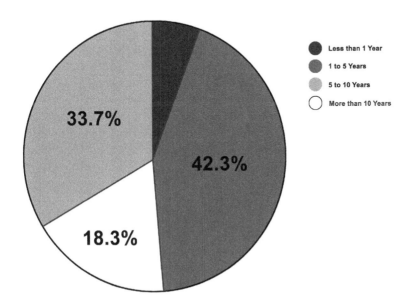

Figure I.2 Great Big Business Librarian Survey: Number of Years in Profession, 2016

broad overview to get you started offering business services. We will examine how public libraries are reaching out to the business community and marketing their services and give you many examples. We will also introduce strategies you can use to start or improve a business service within your library.

We start with the Preface, The Who, What, and Why, which tells a little about how we got to be business librarians. In Chapter 1, The Business Librarian, we will cover the basics of being a business specialist and offering business services. Here we try to give some ideas about becoming a business librarian with lots of help from colleagues. We also cover the basics of the business reference interview and how it may differ from a general reference interview. Chapter 2, Setting Up Your Space, is filled with ideas on how to physically situate the business space in the library to create the biggest impact services. For those of you without physical space to devote, we have included information on creating a virtual space. Chapter 3, At Your Service, covers important advice on getting out there and presenting services to the community. In Chapter 4, Deep in the Data, and Chapter 5, Some of the Best Things in Life. . ., we will introduce some of the best paid and free business resources out there. We've compiled these lists from our own web page as well as from the work we do with other business librarians. They are by no means exhaustive. While we will tend to focus on digital resources, Chapter 6, Old School: A Quick Note on Print, is a brief look at what to consider if building a print collection. Using what's been learned from business reference, Chapter 7, Programming and Special Events, guides readers toward creating programming that complements services. We've included lots of real-life examples from libraries throughout the country. We show in Chapter 8, Reaching Out Is (Not) Hard to Do, how to get the word out about all these great resources, programs, and services you are offering. And finally, we've included some Stories from the Front Line in Chapter 9. These aren't necessarily the stumpers or the wackiest requests we received, but they do illustrate some of the situations we deal with on a daily basis.

Read this book however it works for you—cover to cover or jump around. Each chapter can stand alone. We encourage you to check out the Bibliography for helpful readings.

We love this quote from Bryant McGill:

Whatever makes you uncomfortable is your biggest opportunity for growth.

Throughout this book we will talk about some uncomfortable situations you might be in—tough business reference questions, your first networking event, asking your director for more funds. It's tough, but you will grow and learn from it. And we think you will love it!

CHAPTER 1

The Business Librarian

You know the feeling. Startled from deep slumber by the sounds of the morning traffic report, you hit the "off" button on your alarm and slink out of bed. Still lingering in the grayness between dreams and consciousness, you trudge to the bathroom wondering what the new day will bring. In what seems like a flash, you are now at the employee entrance, holding the door open for your colleagues behind you, making your way through halls of quiet murmuring, and approaching your desk. As you walk, you extend your neck up, over, and around your coworkers' desk so you can just make out a clear view of your phone. No red voicemail light; no voicemails! Your pace now quickens as you sidle up to your desk, with a sense of relief. *Why so nervous about such things?*—you think to yourself. You surely would be able to handle.

Ring Ring.
You've been asked by your supervisor to be the point person for a new and exciting service offered by the library. You have been told that it is necessary in order to "preserve the momentum of the evolution of the library" whatever that means. After years of doing Reader's Advisory and Sci-Fi Book Club, after spending what seemed like weeks in coming up with the most clever-looking bookmark for this year's Summer Reading Club (it's a man diving into a pool shaped like a book—Dive into Reading—brilliant, right?), you've been asked to answer business reference questions.

Ring Ring.
There's a flyer in the lobby with *your* extension on it. It offers access to "business reference services" and "help with industry research,

demographics, and more!" There's a clip art of a man sitting at a desk with a pie chart behind him. You think: *why did they pick me?* You cringe.

Ring Ring.
You consider making it go to voicemail, but that would just delay the inevitable. You consider that job offer to bus tables at a bar in Key West. You've always liked the smell of limes and Jimmy Buffett songs. *You pick up the phone.*

Regardless of our backgrounds, our focus during our graduate work, or where we started, the fact is we are all librarians and are capable of helping anyone asking a business reference question. Both the authors began their work lives in a corporate world, specifically in sales and marketing. Having some idea of what goes on in a company would most certainly help anyone answering these types of questions, but it's not required.

During our research, we spoke to a number of librarians who were in the process of "becoming business librarians" or, more specifically, they were asked by their administration to offer business reference services to support their local business community. There were a number of strikingly common traits among them. Fear was a big one: many of them were thrown into their situation without any previous experience. We were regularly told, "I don't know where to start . . ." and "I have no idea what I should be doing." The simple fact that you are reading this book is a good sign that you are on the right path. Knowing that you are not alone in this endeavor and that even the authors were in the same boat as you are now should be comforting. We'll get you through this.

Frankly, you are more than halfway to becoming a business librarian. Most of what you do for your patrons now is more than enough to get you to where you need to be. The one thing that is most important for you is an understanding of the business reference interview.

In the very first sentence of the preface to her essential book on business reference, *Making Sense of Business Reference*, Celia Ross says it all, "No one is safe from business reference." What's the difference between how one handles a general reference question and a business reference question? Nothing. In our experience, we have seen this as one of the biggest obstacles for nonbusiness librarians. Their response to a business reference question—"Help, I'm not a business librarian!" When moving from a generalist to business specialist, the first thing to always remember is that you are a librarian first and foremost. As librarians we have been taught to guide patrons to the information they need. This is no different when you are helping a business patron. Think about what you know about the reference interview. You are a research professional and you can do this.

You already know how to do a proper reference interview. In many cases, it's fairly simple. A patron comes to you asking for a book on building and maintaining a vegetable garden, so you do a search and find that part of your collection that would be helpful. You might also go a little further and obtain information on growing zones, fertilizers, and weather. Maybe you even go so far as to get a cookbook for him or her to use after his or her harvest.

The reference interview with your average budding entrepreneur will probably not be as simple. The real challenge? Many entrepreneurs only know what they *want*, not what they *need*. The challenge is knowing what they need. Emotion will be a main driver for your business patrons. They have a business idea, one that they are hoping will come to fruition and support them financially. In their eyes, it is the most amazing idea ever. It's going to make them wealthy beyond comprehension.

Here's where it might become tricky. For many reference requests, the outcome of your response will not affect a patron's livelihood. For example, a student may ask you for books on the U.S. involvement in World War I. You might pull some books that address the socioeconomic issues of the time; European history; a book about the sinking of the *Lusitania*, and so forth. Perhaps a patron tells you that he or she enjoys a good mystery, or more specifically, historical fiction. Your reader's advisory experience, along with the wonderful online resources that are available, will lead you and your patron to his or her next read.

Even more helpful is the ability to turn to a coworker and ask for advice: "Hey Jim, I'm not much of a historical fiction reader, any ideas for a good book for this patron?" There are many avenues to go down, and in the end, the patron will be satisfied with the outcome. If something isn't available, or not quite what he or she wanted, there are alternatives.

However, dealing with an entrepreneur or business owner can have different stakes. The entrepreneur has applied for a business loan and the bank requires information on industry and market trends, or he or she won't be considered. Perhaps a small business owner is struggling with sales and needs to find out about the competition, or he or she might go out of business. It's not as cut-and-dried as "Oh, we are out of James Patterson's new book ... let me suggest another author." And since you are most likely just dipping your toes into the business reference pool, you are all alone in this great big world without anyone to ask for advice at your library.

Knowing patrons are coming to you because they need assistance to start, grow, or continue their business could add some stress to your reference interview, and rightfully so. This idea alone may discourage you, but it shouldn't stop you. Business librarians are an important part of a much bigger picture. The services and resources you provide will not only be a part of supporting small business owners, but it will also become a key component in steps entrepreneurs take to make their small businesses successful.

So yes, there will be some initial pressure when you move over to business reference. It doesn't have to feel that way, though. Simply familiarizing yourself with the small business world will help. So try doing a few of these, and flex those brain muscles of yours.

- Browse the Business sections of national and your local newspapers.

- *New York Times Business Day* is a great source for daily business and finance news and information. There are separate sections for Money, Media, Technology, and even Entrepreneurship. http:// www.nytimes.com/pages/business/index.html.

- *Wall Street Journal* has separate sections for Business and Economics. Within the Business section, there is a dedicated Entrepreneurship section, which focuses on items of interest to entrepreneurs and small business owners. For instance, while making last-minute edits to this book, I checked the site again and found a great article entitled "Why We Need to Tell Different Stories about Entrepreneurs" that discussed the myth of the uber-successful sole entrepreneur (Aarons-Mele 2016). As a business librarian, it gave me some insight into the pressure entrepreneurs may put on themselves. Are they gauging their success through millions of dollars in sales and IPOs? Are these unrealistic standards setting them up to fail? http://www.wsj.com/.

- We are lucky to have a dedicated business newspaper, *Long Island Business News*, that really helps us stay connected with local business news, data, and trends. Check out your area for any dedicated business news sources. http://www.libn.com.

- Even if your area doesn't have a dedicated business paper, your local paper may have a business section. Our area paper, *Newsday*, has several pages dedicated to Long Island business and economy. Familiarize yourself with the section and the journalists covering the beat; maybe they'll do a story on your new business center. http:// www.newsday.com/business.

- Know what business titles are on the business or nonfiction best-seller lists:
  - *Wall Street Journal.* http://www.wsj.com/public/page/news-books -best-sellers.html.
  - *USA Today.* http://www.usatoday.com/life/books/best-selling/.

- Flip through some business magazines such as *Inc.*, *Entrepreneur*, and *Forbes*. Check out their websites too.

- Keep an eye on the business networks both on TV and online: CNN Money, CNBC, Fox Business, Bloomberg.

- Read a few "classic" business books. Some of our favorites are *Who Moved My Cheese?* by Spencer Johnson; *The Seven Habits of Highly Successful People* by Stephen Covey; and *How to Win Friends and Influence People* by Dale Carnegie. Not sure those are the best books for your needs?

- A book like *The 100 Best Business Books of All Time: What They Say, Why They Matter, and How They Can Help You* by Jack Covert and Todd Satterstein can help with overviews of the most popular topics. Newly revised, the update includes 100 business books, separated by topic, with reviews. Hoping to capture the themes and ideas behind some business books without reading them all? Try a book like *The Best Business Books Ever: The Most Influential Management Books You'll Never Have Time to Read.* While the focus is on management, the titles in this compendium run the gamut. Each entry includes the book's contribution to management, its key themes, important points, and further readings.

- Check out *Inc.*'s "7 Short Books worth More than an MBA" for books covering success, finance, innovation, management, and sales (James 2015). The title of the article is not misleading. These books are truly short and inspiring reads and will put you well on your way to understanding the entrepreneurial mind.

- Read books (besides this one) about business reference.

- *Making Sense of Business Reference: A Guide for Librarians and Research Professionals* is a comprehensive guide to performing business reference. Its author, Celia Ross, guides users through many different reference scenarios and includes a variety of free and subscription resources to answer even the toughest business reference questions.

- *Small Business and the Public Library: Strategies of a Successful Partnership*, coauthored by Elizabeth Malafi, guides librarians through business reference and services through the work of the Miller Center at the Middle Country Public Library and several other libraries from around the country.

- *Strauss's Handbook of Business Information: A Guide for Librarians, Students and Researchers* by Rita W. Moss and David G. Ernsthausen is now in its third edition and continues to be an indispensable guide for all in the business reference field.

Now you are ready!

As librarians, we know from experience that a good reference interview is the key to all successful reference transactions. Listen carefully, and ask questions for clarification until you are comfortable and understand what the patron wants.

Many of the librarians we spoke to while writing this book have told us that their most asked business reference question is simply "I want to start a business, what do I do?" Sonya Durney of Portland Public Library said that most new entrepreneurs come in and say "I don't even know where to start." In his book, *The Customer Rules: The 39 Essential Rules for Delivering Sensational Service*, Lee Cockerell writes, "Great companies and successful individuals alike keep a keen eye on the basics at all times." His rule #4 "Don't get bored with the basics" holds so true for all types of librarians and is worth remembering when you are answering this typical question again.

When asked about this typical business reference question, Bryce Thornton, from the Hoover Public Library in Hoover, Alabama, responded, "Each question is different, that is what makes work exciting for me." This sentiment is so important for all librarians to remember and even more so, business librarians. The most popular business reference question might be, "How do I start a business?" but each of those budding entrepreneurs will have a different idea in their heads. It might be the thousandth time you have been asked this question, but it's that person's first time asking it. They are putting themselves in your hands.

Here it is. Your first reference question as a business librarian. *Don't panic.* Start with a resource you know. Then try another resource you know. Go through each of the resources you know, and see what you come up with.

Don't feel like you have to get the answer immediately. Sometimes we need more time to research the answer. Other times we are too busy with other patrons to devote the energy and time a question might need. Maybe we don't even know how to get the information. You're mentally reviewing all your databases and other go-to resources, but nothing is sparking an idea. Now what?

Don't worry. Hope is not all lost. There are many avenues you can take to get an answer.

Ask your fellow business librarians. We encourage you to create a network of business librarians. Perhaps there is a local or statewide group of business librarians you can turn to for help.

The ALA RUSA Business Reference and Services Section, or BRASS, is invaluable especially if there isn't a local or state group of business librarians in your area. This group consists of academic, corporate, public, and business librarians, and as stated on their website, BRASS is "your station for all aspects of business reference." The website (http://www.ala.org/rusa/

sections/brass) contains many helpful business reference resources, including Business LibGuides, Best of the Best Business Websites, Public Librarians Toolkit, and more. All are maintained by business librarians who are active in the organization.

Check out the library websites of business schools. They often include valuable subject-specific Lib-Guides. Some that have helped us are the following:

- BRASS Libguides: http://brass.libguides.com/.
- Yale Business and Management Research Guide: http://guides.library.yale.edu/business.
- Michigan State University Entrepreneurship and Small Business: http://libguides.lib.msu.edu/entrepreneur.
- Join the BusLib e-mail group. Not only can you ask for help answering your stumpers, but you can also see what other librarians are struggling with and maybe even help! You can subscribe at http://lists.nau.edu/cgi-bin/wa?A0=BUSLIB-L.
- Use the #bizref on social media to ask fellow business librarians for help.

Here's the great thing about doing business research: the more you do it and the more you help the small business owners, the more you will understand what they need and where they are coming from. We can't mention how many times a new patron comes in with a reference question that is exactly what a patron two months ago asked. Frankly, most small business owners are going to ask you the same thing: How can I find customers? What's my competition doing? Who's my competition? Aren't you warm wearing that cardigan when it's 80° outside?

Granted, there will be times when a small business owner will come to you with a real whopper of a question. The first time someone asks you a question with an industry term or business term that you've never heard before, you'll probably feel intimidated. It's OK. We've been doing this for over 10 years: we still get requests that make our head spin. We still bounce ideas off of our colleagues on a daily basis. Prepare yourself to be asked for things you've never heard of, things that clearly you do not have access to, things that don't exist in this universe, and downright ridiculous things. Take it all in stride, and be conscious of these requests.

But still, there comes a time when you may exhaust all these resources and still have a hard time coming up with the answer. *Shh!* We are going to tell you a not-so-secret secret. One you probably know already. One that is true for almost every reference subject. Ready? Not every business reference question can be answered. There. We said it. Sometimes there is just not an answer. Or maybe the answer is a trade secret. When this is the case, we often try to offer some sort of information that might not be the answer but is close. Or the closest we can get.

According to Reference and User Services Association's (RUSA) *Guidelines for Behavioral Performance of Reference and Information Service Providers*, "The positive or negative behavior of the librarian (as observed by the patron) becomes a significant factor in perceived success or failure" (RUSA 2011). Getting the closest answer that you can generally results in a positive interaction for the patron.

Once you begin to get your bearings as the library's business librarian, you should consider sharing your knowledge with your colleagues. In doing so, you know your business patrons will receive assistance even if you are not available.

There are a number of ways you can create a more comfortable environment for someone working the business services desk or even just answering business reference questions. Like anything else that is new, there will be a learning curve. Your best approach would be to not take on the whole business reference world right from the start. Focus on the simpler reference subjects.

Guidebook

Every reference desk should have an in-house guidebook to business reference. Get a three-hole binder, and label it accordingly. Fill it with pages of useful information such as:

A listing of your subscription databases and detailed descriptions of what they offer;

A list of frequently asked reference questions and answers, along with what resource was used to find the answer;

Important phone numbers to your community's business organizations (Chamber of Commerce, SBDC, SCORE, Rotary, SBA office);

A reference log (See Figure 1.1): a table in which anyone who answers a business reference question must log the request, including the solution; and

Of course, your extension number!

Wiki

Wiki? Why not! Have a web-savvy member on your staff who can help set up an online wiki? Put him or her to good use. Most wikis are free, plug-and-play services that will allow you to create one in minutes. Best of all,

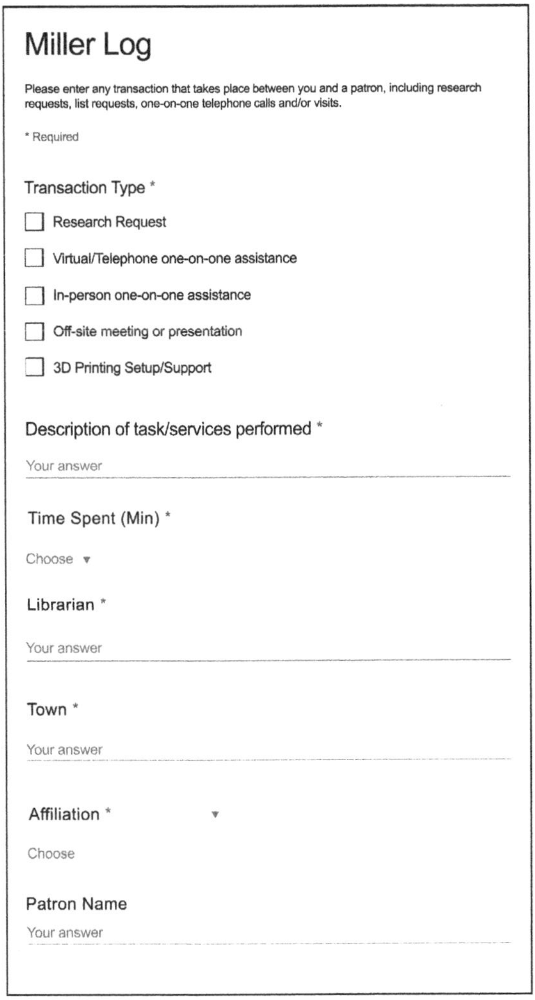

Miller Log

Please enter any transaction that takes place between you and a patron, including research requests, list requests, one-on-one telephone calls and/or visits.

* Required

Transaction Type *

☐ Research Request

☐ Virtual/Telephone one-on-one assistance

☐ In-person one-on-one assistance

☐ Off-site meeting or presentation

☐ 3D Printing Setup/Support

Description of task/services performed *

Your answer

Time Spent (Min) *

Choose ▾

Librarian *

Your answer

Town *

Your answer

Affiliation *   ▾

Choose

Patron Name

Your answer

Figure 1.1. Example of an online business reference log.

most wikis will come with built-in features such as keyword search. Organize your common reference questions and their respective solutions on one page, and use the search feature to find what you are looking for. Link your wiki from your intranet for easy access.

In-House Training

You've heard this before: seeing is believing and practice makes perfect. The more business reference questions you answer, the better you will become at finding answers. Setting up in-house training sessions on using your various resources will add an additional comfort level to all staff when answering these types of questions. Once you feel comfortable in your role, consider offering quick introductions and more in-depth reviews of the library's business services and resources. An hour's worth of training few times a year can do wonders toward improving the comfort level of your staff. Even better: have cookies or some sort of danish along with coffee and tea. Librarians dig danish. You know you do.

Subscription Database Training

Subscribe to a subscription database? Take advantage of any offer of training from your vendors. The more comfortable you are using your electronic resources, the better you can serve your patrons. In most cases, these are webinars in which a representative from the database will guide you through the features and process of doing research. Invite your coworkers, too. Vendors usually will offer this training to your patrons as well. Don't be surprised if the vendor offers to send someone to your site to do in-person training; it's in their best interest to encourage usage, and it's to your advantage. (See Chapter 7, Programming and Special Events, for more on this.)

Computer Skills Training

We think it's safe to say that most of you are handy with a computer. However, having a general understanding of how to use spreadsheet software such as Microsoft Excel or Google Sheets is almost certainly required. Much of what you will be doing in way of data gathering will involve a spreadsheet. CSV files, also known as Comma Separated Value files, will open in any spreadsheet software and are the most commonly used format for downloading lists and data files. Knowing how to sort data, copy and paste columns, combine columns, and navigate through rows of data will come in handy. While many business librarians we've spoken to do not do the actual downloading and compiling of data, patrons may ask you how it's done.

You have a number of options to brush up on your computer skills. Microsoft offers a great deal of online help and how-to pages in their online Knowledgebase (Microsoft 2015). Google offers a Learning Center for their apps that will walk you through Sheets (Google 2016a). You'll also be able to find a number of instructional videos on YouTube. If your library subscribes to a service like Lynda.com or Universal Class, you can spend a few hours learning everything you need to know about using Microsoft Excel or any spreadsheet program. You do not have to be an expert at this, but it will help with any frustration you may experience when doing research or helping your patrons download data. Most other data you'll find online are in either PDF format or text document.

A quick note on other computer skills you may need: if you are doing the marketing for business services, knowledge of using publishing software such as Microsoft Publisher will come in handy. Again, there are plenty of online resources for you to learn how to use it. Your creative style and writing ability are all up to you. We'll give you some ideas in Chapter 8, Reaching Out Is (Not) Hard to Do.

Stay Organized

Here's a great tip on keeping things organized in your business center: use the free resources provided by Google! Google Docs and Forms are amazing tools that are easy to use and will come in handy if you have a small (or no) budget. One practical use is to create a program registration form.

It will be necessary for you to set up an account in Google. If you already have a Gmail account, you can access your Google Drive account by visiting http://drive.google.com. When creating any document, you will have the option of sharing it with other members of your team by entering their e-mail address and assigning them different levels of access. Users can edit, comment, or view the data. Editors will have access to all the data, including the form's design. Viewers will be able to see the results of your registrations but not be able to edit the contents of the form or the results spreadsheet.

It is important when setting up your sharing options to make sure to share the results file. This is the file created by Google Drive to collect your responses and is labeled as such. Since the information is collected by Google and compiled into a handy spreadsheet, it can be edited, manipulated, and exported to your liking.

The many benefits of using Google Drive does not stop at program registration. If you have access to a tablet, smartphone, or laptop for your program, you can check in attendees as they arrive right from your registration spreadsheet and even add those pesky drop-in patrons on the fly.

Now that you've had success in taking registrations, sharing that information with your programming department, and using your list to check in attendees on the fly, what else can you do? How about a follow-up? Since you have the e-mail addresses of your attendees, why not survey them on the program they attended? In addition to text fields and drop-down menus, Google Drive allows you to add scales to allow your patrons to rate their instructor, let you know what they may be interested in as far as future programs, or let you know how easy it was to register for your program!

Once you have designed your form and are ready to start accepting responses, you will have the option of either embedding it into an existing web page (which may require some web design know-how) or making it a web link. Google also allows you to share your form using various social networking outlets such as Facebook and Google+. When a patron visits the link, he or she is forwarded directly to your online form. Since this link is unique and permanent, you have the option of editing your existing form at any time without having to change your web link. The possibilities are endless and the price is right.

Do-It-Yourself Website

Finally, let's talk about your web presence. You may or may not have control over your business services web page, but it is incredibly important that you and your administrators know that in all likelihood, if small business owners hear about the services you provide, the first place they are going to seek you out is online. Don't worry about having the most attractive website out there; what's necessary here is usefulness and relevance.

If you are not a website designer or do not have access to one, don't fret. If you know how to use software such as Microsoft Office, you could probably put together a simple blog site using WordPress or one of the many other free online services.

We are guessing that in most cases, you will have to host your online presence through your library's own website, and that's fine. Believe it or not, just one page worth of web space on your library's site is enough to get you started. Believe us, once your library director sees how much traffic your business reference services page is getting, you'll have a case to get some more web space and perhaps your own dedicated site.

Free Blog Services

- **WordPress** (www.wordpress.com)—By far the largest of the blogging platforms, WordPress comprises almost 16 million websites on the web, and over 76 million blogs can be found on the company's free WordPress.com hosting service. The nice thing about WordPress is that it's incredibly flexible and offers users of varying degrees of technical prowess and the ability to set up and maintain an attractive looking site. If you wish to host your blog on your library's website, it will be necessary to install WordPress on your server. Once it is installed, you will be able to create user accounts. This comes in handy if you have multiple people editing or managing the site. You can assign users with different levels of access from administrator to editor. Users will log into WordPress from their web browsers. WordPress has a fairly easy-to-use interface along with a dashboard that keeps all aspects of your site within easy reach. If you or your colleagues are savvy with a browser and know how to use a word processor, you shouldn't have any issues managing your blog. WordPress can also be used as a Content Management System. It is the basis of many websites on the web: it may not look like WordPress or your typical blog, but in many cases, it is.

- **Tumblr** (www.tumblr.com)—Owned by Yahoo!, Tumblr is a free blogging service that leans more toward sharing images, audio, and video. Its real strength is its ease of use: there is not much here to the "back end," as Tumblr in its purest form is a blog and not much else. There are ways to customize the look and feel of your blog using Tumblr, but not to the extent available using WordPress. Tumblr is popular: There are about 324 million blogs, and folks post over 40 million posts per day.

- **Blogger** (www.blogger.com)—Google's simple blogging platform is easy to use but requires some HTML knowledge if you wish to customize. There are a number of ready-to-use and free templates available, so if you are not particular, you will be able to find something appropriate for your site. If your organization or you are big Google users (Mail, Calendar, Drive), this is a good choice, since it will utilize a single log-on and the ability to easily insert Google elements.

- **Weebly** (www.weebly.com)—Using a widget-based approach, Weebly is a free, simple blog platform that offers a lot of hand-holding for the nontechie types. If you have zero experience, this would be the place to start. Free and simple comes with a price: you will have very little opportunity to customize your blog to be exactly what you want, but it will most certainly be better than nothing at all. Like other free blog sites, the service will require that your blog is hosted on their domain, which will be something you'll have to seriously consider. For example, users will visit mybizlibrary.weebly.com instead of mybizlibrary.com, which you'd have to pay for if you use a custom domain with their service.

No matter what your skill level is, you are a business librarian *right now*, and you are a business librarian the moment you commit to helping the entrepreneurs and the small business community. Once you make that commitment, you will begin your training (hopefully utilizing this book) and never end.

Remember This

Once you commit to helping your business community, you are a business librarian. Own that title and be proud of it. You have joined a vibrant community!

CHAPTER 2

Setting Up
Your Space

You are ready to bring business into the library! Now it is time to consider what space you can offer within the library. Big or small, rural or urban, fear not budding business librarians, there are endless options available to you when determining where to set up a business space. In this chapter, we'll look at some options—physical and virtual. Yes! There are many options for those without space to dedicate to business services; have no fear, the web is here!

Let's say your director has given you the go-ahead to start off small. You procure some shelf space and start to build your business collection. Naming your collection will help distinguish it from the general nonfiction and will also lend credibility to the library's business services. It doesn't have to be anything flashy—business collection is a good start. Naming it will help patrons know that it exists. Signage will be important. If you've pulled the business titles out of the general nonfiction collection, a shelf-talker guiding patrons to the new location will help. If possible, create or purchase labels for the business titles so they stand out.

The Desk

Shelf space is working out and the director is ready to have a dedicated desk. The most effective placement would be next to your business collection. We know that many patrons never visit the reference desk or even ask for help. They often browse the stacks hoping the book or subject they are searching for will catch their eye. Being there when the patron comes upon your business collection will allow you to offer immediate assistance. If possible, add a dedicated phone with extension to this area.

The Corner

Let's face it: having a dedicated desk alone will be a great marketing tool for your services, but as business services grow you may need a little more breathing room. There might not be much space to work with, but what would be great in this scenario is a few sets of bookshelves, a periodicals counter, a brochure stand, table and chairs, and a small reference desk.

Stock your bookshelves with a well-rounded collection of business titles, very little of which would be considered reference, and be sure to offer popular titles, such as the *Wall Street Journal* best sellers, and books that focus on the needs of the small business owners you are working with on a day-to-day basis. Your periodicals shelf should have a few national business magazines and trade papers as well as some business newspapers. Check out what other business libraries are offering.

You should make sure that your brochure stand is always stocked with your program flyers as well as ones that focus on your services and online databases. If possible, market this area as a dedicated space for business reference services. If you have a table, use it for one-on-one appointments with patrons as well as offering a spot for patrons to do business research. Make sure your desk looks over the entire space, allowing you to keep an eye on your patrons and assist them if necessary while you do work such as updating your website or doing business research.

As you continue to grow, approach your director for the extra space and resources you will need: extra shelving, seating, brochure holders. You are your own best advocate, and the more help you provide your patrons, the more the word will get out.

The Center

As the business services continue to grow, you may need a dedicated space where local small business owners, students of business, up-and-coming entrepreneurs, and everyone in between can find support for their businesses. The dedicated space can host a modest collection of print materials, both circulating and reference, as well as a common area with tables and chairs for patrons to sit and do research, read, study, and so on. Dedicated computers for patron use, specifically for doing business research, will entice people to spend time in the library. If possible, set aside a small group of offices that can be used for one-on-one appointments and perhaps for local businesses to reserve as well and dedicated areas for programming, where you may offer business seminars, computer workshops, and even networking events. If possible, offer coworking space for local entrepreneurs. It doesn't have to be a private room, just a space where businesspeople can gather and collaborate.

A center of this size requires a team, so plan accordingly. Team members should rotate through desk shifts, programming blocks, and one-on-one appointments.

There's a step up from the "center," and it's truly amazing. Remarkable in its size and scope, Library 21c is a great example of the future of business librarianship. When Pikes Peak Library District wanted to expand their business services to their small business owners in their community, they went big, very big. A former MCI call center building was transformed into Library 21c, an incredible resource for the community, which takes the notion of "business center" to a grand scale. About 71,000 square feet is dedicated to patrons, offering abundant opportunities to research, build, and run their businesses.

Library 21c offers meeting spaces, computers, an exhibition space with room for 400, access to over 100 subscription databases, and a Makerspace that includes 3D printers, laser cutters, sewing machines and tools. Patrons can also get a bite to eat at the cafe on-site. Library 21c is just one part of the sprawling 14-branch Pikes Peak Library District, serving 285,000 library users.

One large component of Library 21c is their ability to offer meeting spaces for businesses. Known as hoteling, the library offers a wide selection of sizes and amenities. From something as simple as a desk and Wi-Fi to exhibit space that can accommodate up to 400 attendees, patrons have access to such things as whiteboards, conference rooms, classrooms for training, and computers with software for graphic designing, publishing, writing, and accessing subscription databases. Amazingly, there is no fee to use the facilities.

While anyone can use the space (including "for-profit" companies), "sales, sales pitches, or general business" is prohibited at the library and must be done off-site. Companies can most certainly follow up with attendees with the ultimate goal of doing business with patrons, but that transaction must take place afterward.

Library 21c's Makerspaces are equally impressive. 3D printers, laser cutters, sewing machines, computers, electronic components, and drawers filled with tools are available to any small business owner looking to prototype or create his or her product. Pikes Peak requires that any patron using their Makerspace go through a vetting process, including training sessions, before he or she is signed off to use the equipment in the Makerspace. After going through this process, the patron's records are updated to indicate that he or she is eligible to use the space. Additionally, at least one staff member is on hand to supervise the operation.

This brings us to this important note on Makerspaces: it is incredibly important that you or someone in your organization is committed to managing it. Offering these amazing tools and services could very well be a full-time job. Library 21c has a very clear policy and procedure in place for those wanting to use their Makerspace. (See Figure 2.1.)

In addition to meeting spaces and Makerspace, Library 21c has a copy center on-site, managed by RICOH. Chosen through an RFP (Request for Proposal) process, the copy center is a full-service location. Patrons can also get a bite to eat at the Her Story Cafe, also operated by an outside

Makerspace Use Agreement and Release of Liability for Adult Patrons (the "Agreement")

The Pikes Peak Library District (PPLD) provides patrons with the opportunity to use its Makerspace facilities and equipment, as described in more detail below. All patron use of Makerspace facilities and equipment is entirely optional and voluntary and is for purposes of recreation, education, and/or self-improvement.

In order to use the Makerspace facilities and equipment, each adult user (a patron who is aged 18 or older) ("Adult User") must review this Agreement, provide the Adult User information requested in Section 1 below, and sign and comply with this Agreement. If the adult user has a legal guardian or other person legally responsible to sign documents such as this, the guardian/legally responsible person must sign in the space designated below.

Please note that this document includes a Release of Liability that releases PPLD and others related to it from liability for personal injuries and other losses resulting from the Adult User's use of the Makerspace facilities and equipment. Please read carefully.

1. **Adult User Information**

   Name_____
   Library Card #_____
   Driver's License/Student ID #_____ School (if using student ID)_____
   Phone #_____ Email_____
   Address_____
   Emergency Contact Name, Address and Telephone Number:_____
   _____

2. **Conditions of Use.** By signing below, the Adult User affirms and agrees that: (1) he/she is capable of participating in the Makerspace Activities (as defined below); (2) the Adult User shall comply with all PPLD policies and procedures, including all Makerspace policies, guidelines, and instructions; (3) Adult User shall be responsible to pay any PPLD charges or fees for use of Makerspace tools, equipment and materials, and for damage, loss or clean-up of PPLD property, which may be valued and billed to Adult User's PPLD account or by other means, in PPLD's discretion; and (4) all insurance of Adult User applicable to any injuries or claims arising out of the Makerspace Activities (defined below) shall be primary with any applicable PPLD insurance being secondary.

3. **Makerspace Activities; Assumption of Risk.** PPLD's Makerspace facilities and equipment include, but are not limited to, video production equipment, recording devices, drawing tools and equipment, circuit boards, electrical wiring, electronic equipment, saws, drills, screwdrivers, routers, wood- and metal working tools, 3-dimensional copying and printing machines, computer equipment, charging stations, and wood, metal, plastic and composite supplies and materials, glue, solvents, nails, screws, and other working parts. While most tools, equipment, and supplies will be provided by PPLD, on occasion such items will be supplied by users. Adult User may work alone or share Makerspace work space, tools and equipment with other users and PPLD staff. PPLD may require users to wear specified safety gear, and undergo training, but safety gear and training may not always be available. Surfaces of floors, work benches and tables in Makerspace areas may have debris, dust, liquids, and sharp objects. While PPLD will strive to supervise Makerspace areas, not all activities of Adult User or other users can be supervised at all times. All above-referenced and other use of Makerspace work areas, facilities, tools, and equipment, whether alone or with others, whether supervised or not, and whether performed according to PPLD policies, procedures, and safety rules, or not, shall be referred to as the "Makerspace Activities."

FIGURE 2.1 A great example of a Makerspace User Agreement from the Pikes Peak Library District.

The undersigned Adult User understands and agrees that the Makerspace Activities involve various hazards, dangers, and risks, including without limitation, and by way of example, the risk of trips, slips and falls; cuts, broken bones, burns, and other wounds to hands, head, feet, eyes and other body parts; electrical shock; exposure to dust, fumes, smoke, noise, and vibrations; and accidents due to negligence of other users or PPLD staff or vendors, or due to defective or inadequate facilities, equipment, tools, machinery, or due to inadequate maintenance or repair, training, instructions, supervision, first aid and medical treatment, or safety gear. The risks also include other risks arising from Adult User's involvement in the Makerspace Activities, including unpredictable risks and risks inherent in the use of the work areas, facilities, tools and equipment used in Makerspace Activities. Each Adult User agrees that such Adult User's participation in Makerspace Activities involves risks of accidents and serious personal injury and illness, paralysis, permanent disability, and even possibly death, of the Adult User. All above-referenced risks and other risks arising from the Makerspace Activities are referred to herein as the "Risks."

The undersigned Adult User expressly assumes, for such Adult User, and for such Adult User's heirs, family and estate, executors, administrators, assigns, and personal representatives, all Risks arising from the Adult User's participation in Makerspace Activities, whether those Risks are known or unknown, or are predictable or unpredictable, or are Risks inherent in the Makerspace Activities.

4. **Release of Liability and Indemnification of Claims of Adult User:** In consideration for the privilege granted to the Adult User to participate in the Makerspace Activities, and with full awareness and appreciation of the Risks involved, the undersigned Adult User, for and on behalf of the Adult User and Adult User's heirs, family and estate, executors, administrators, assigns, and personal representatives, hereby releases and agrees to indemnify and hold harmless PPLD, its Board of Trustees, and all organizations related to PPLD, including the Friends of the Pikes Peak Library District and the PPLD Foundation, and PPLD's and its related organizations' affiliates, directors, officers, trustees, employees, volunteers, contractors, agents, representatives and successors and assigns (the "Released Parties") of and from any and all claims, demands, liabilities, and causes of action that may arise from or could be made against or incurred by the Released Parties or any of them with respect to any and all property damage, economic loss, medical expense, personal care expense, disability, disease, personal injury or illness whether physical or mental in nature, and/or death, whether caused by negligence or otherwise, suffered by the Adult User and arising from the Adult User's participation in the Makerspace Activities, and the Risks, including all claims of the undersigned Adult User. This Release and Indemnification includes all damages, costs, expenses, attorneys' fees, and economic and other losses which may be sought in any such claims.

5. **Consent to Medical Treatment.** If the Adult User is injured or becomes ill while involved in Makerspace Activities, the Adult User hereby authorizes PPLD and its employees, volunteers, agents and representatives to obtain and consent to, on the Adult User's behalf, medical care, including without limitation, medical treatment, hospitalization, ambulance transportation, anesthesia, and X-ray and other exams and tests. The undersigned Adult User agrees to pay all costs of such medical care and transportation.

6. **Miscellaneous. The Adult User agrees that PPLD provides no warranties of merchantability or fitness for particular purpose or use concerning any project or items made using PPLD equipment, tools or materials.** If any provision of this document is determined to be invalid for any reason, such invalidity shall not affect the validity of any other provisions, which other provisions shall remain in full force and effect as if this Agreement had been executed with the invalid provision eliminated. By signing below the undersigned person agrees that this document is intended to be as broad and inclusive as permitted under applicable law. This document is governed by Colorado law, and any claims brought concerning it must be commenced in the state courts of El Paso County, Colorado, or the U.S. District Court for

FIGURE 2.1 (Continued)

company. The library's exhibit space, known as Venue@21c, can accommodate 400 people. About 60 percent of the space is utilized by outside organizations. The balance is used for in-house programming and events. For example, 21c librarian Terry Zarksy created a Business Resource Fair, in which 40 vendors participated, including the local Small Business Development Center, SCORE, and government agencies. Patrons who are starting businesses will be able to attend and interact with representatives from the various organizations all under one roof.

In contrast to the relatively new concept of Library 21c, another long-standing institution is doing their part to support local businesses using a more traditional approach. Sitting in the shadow of the Empire State Building, the Science, Industry and Business Library of the New York Public

Colorado. This document shall not be amended except by a written document signed by the Adult User and the Executive Director of PPLD.

By my signature below, I acknowledge that I have carefully read this Agreement in its entirety and understand it, and I voluntarily agree to all statements and provisions of this Agreement, including the Release of Liability and Indemnification of Section 4. I am sufficiently informed about the Makerspace Activities and Risks involved to decide whether to sign this Agreement. I attest that I am eighteen (18) years of age or older.

Adult User Signature:

Signature_____

Date_____

Printed name_____

By my signature below, I acknowledge that I am a legal guardian or other person legally responsible for the Adult User with authority to sign this Agreement for and on behalf of the Adult User. I have carefully read this Agreement in its entirety and understand it, and I voluntarily agree to all statements and provisions of this Agreement, including the Release of Liability and Indemnification of Section 4, for and on behalf of the Adult User. I am sufficiently informed about the Makerspace Activities and Risks involved to decide whether to sign this Agreement for the Adult User. I attest that I am eighteen (18) years of age or older.

Legal Guardian/Legally Responsible Person Signature:

Signature_____

Date_____

Printed name_____

FIGURE 2.1 (Continued)

Library (NYPL) could be intimidating to a small town business librarian. Enter the Madison Avenue doors and be greeted by a large, two-story atrium in a semicircle with brushed nickel accents, where a billboard of sorts is displayed with quotes from pioneers of business and industry. Looking beyond the lobby, you'll see banks of computers surrounded on the outer perimeter by shelves of books. Walk downstairs past various flat-screen TVs showing business channels, and go deeper into great rooms after rooms of computers, shelves of books, offices with windows looking out onto the floor, and patrons going about their businesses. The space is impressive.

Equally impressive is the scope of the resources that are available to patrons here. Listen, it's the NYPL: they offer practically every business database to patrons, albeit the majority of them are "in-house" only. They also offer office space to SCORE and career counselors every day of the week. And that seems to be the focus: NYPL is active in bringing outside groups in to provide support services to small businesses and individuals. Whereas some business librarians we spoke to do actual research and compiling of data for patrons, the business librarians at NYPL provide more of a nurturing, guiding approach. "The Librarian is not the access point, now the teaching point," says Betty Lacy, assistant head of Collection Services at the NYPL Business Library.

Virtual Services

While having a desk, shelving, programming space, and offices is nice, it is not required. You can be a valuable addition to the business community with a virtual presence: business databases and websites are available to your patrons from their own locations; reference assistance can be done via phone or e-mail; and, remember you should be getting out of the library often. It's important not to hide behind your web page and your resources. You are still a business librarian in this scenario, and it will be important for you to get out there and market yourself, your services, and your online resources.

Operating mainly as a virtual space means you must be all-in with your website. This is your only means of access for your patrons. It should look fantastic and be easy to navigate. Your big ticket items, your business databases, should be front and center, along with information on upcoming programs and your contact information.

Think about publishing at least twice a week on your site. An article focusing on a variety of subjects of interest to small business owners and budding entrepreneurs in the community is a great start. These articles must be informative, sometimes downright entertaining, and many times will be the means of driving traffic to your resources. Attach a social networking component to everything you do. When you publish a new article, make sure to post it on your Twitter or Facebook feed.

Web analytics will show the number of visits and usage of the business databases. Probably the easiest way to accomplish this is to use Google Analytics. Set up a free account and link the website pages that you wish to monitor by copying and pasting Google's text into your website's code. You will then have the option of adding additional metrics to your site. For example, at the Miller Business Center, we have a page where all our databases are listed. Each individual database link is tagged with a Google Analytics code (also known as an "event"). When a user clicks on the link to access your subscription database, it will be logged in your account. You can share your Analytics data with your coworkers or administration by adding "users" to your account.

Another option, especially if you are using a website designed in Word-Press, is the Jetpack plug-in. Jetpack similarly will monitor and count how many times someone clicks on a specific link on your WordPress page. You will be able to run reports right from your WordPress account as well as see a graphical representation of your website's traffic from your WordPress dashboard.

Although virtual, it is important that you be part of everything that happens. Field reference questions via phone and e-mail, and sometimes do one-on-one appointments on the library's public floor. Get the word out so folks know that you are just a click away.

As you can see, the business library and the services you will provide are scalable. While it may seem daunting, you should take careful consideration when planning your space. The last thing you want to do is over-extend your budget or your resources when it is not necessary. Starting small while you build a model that will be the perfect partner for your business community will ensure a successful business center.

Remember This

Don't be daunted by your budget, no matter how small.
It is possible to have a vibrant business space on any budget.

CHAPTER 3

At Your Service

Providing the absolute best service should be your number one priority. Whether your budget allows for the top business databases or you use free information from the government, your patrons will both appreciate and value whatever you offer—as long as you provide consistent and thorough service. Service includes more than just answering reference questions. As librarians we are constantly offering service, not only through reference questions, which we discussed earlier, but also through our resources, programs, and presentations, when we are at outside events, and when we meet with our partners. It's all service, and while it may be part of basic library offerings, it is crucial. Remember Cockerell's Rule #4 "Don't get bored with the basics."

Library Cards for Local Businesses

We are good at getting individuals to sign up for library cards. We have library card sign-up month and promote all the wonderful doors a library card opens for its user. We need to do the same for businesses and entrepreneurs. If you are going to have business services at the library, then you must offer them library cards (See Figure 3.1). Many libraries offer cards with proof of business and other identification. Consider extending resources and services to company employees with prior authorization from the business owner. Requirements should fit within your library guidelines and may even be more restrictive than what is offered to individual patrons. Perhaps, business card holders can only attend business programs and check out business titles. Do what is best for your library while also extending service to your area's economic engine. Having a posted policy is essential. Below is a sample policy from the Hoover Library in Hoover, Alabama (Hoover 2016).

One-On-One Reference

We said it in our introduction and throughout the book and we will say it again—libraries are always changing. One change we have seen in the past few years is the call for more one-on-one reference assistance. These reference interactions are usually preplanned appointments that last 30 minutes—an hour sometimes or more. Often the entrepreneur is looking for general reference assistance. The appointments can include tutorials of popular business databases or an industry review and can help setting up a social media account.

The Miller Business Center began offering one-on-one appointments in response to the many questions they would get after social media programs. Due to demand, the business librarians were offering many programs focusing on different social media platforms—Facebook, Instagram, Twitter, LinkedIn—but learned that while attendees found the programs informative and valuable, they still couldn't get past the point of actually setting up an account. One-on-one appointments began to help get entrepreneurs started.

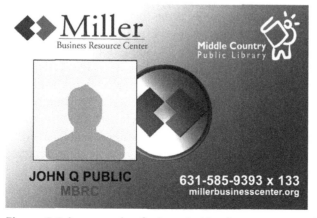

Figure 3.1 An example of a branded business center card.

Many of the librarians we spoke while writing this book have told us that one-on-one appointments have become more and more important to the services they offer. For Julie Kittredge of the Arlington Heights Memorial Library, educating with programs and one-on-one appointments has become a big focus of her job as a business services advisor. The appointments run for an hour and "99% are establishing social media accounts and using them as a marketing tool." One-on-one appointments are an important part of the work Sonya Durney does with Portland Public Library's (PPL) local business population. She usually has about three appointments a week. Jay Lyman at the Seattle Public Library says they do a lot of one-on-one appointments for business patrons throughout the year and that the number keeps growing. In 2016, they offered more than 140. Most, he says, are focused on doing market research for a business or marketing plan.

Having that opportunity to personally chat with a business about their information needs allows you to really promote the databases and services that will help them the most.

Personalized reference services like this are a vital expression of your business services. You are the face of the business services and should strive to connect with businesses as much as possible. Ultimately meeting one-on-one is an opportunity to strengthen your relationships with business patrons.

Partnerships

An article from the March 1, 2016, issue of *Library Journal* entitled "Top Skills for Tomorrow's Librarians" listed the essential competencies for librarians in the next 20 years. Number two on the list is collaboration. "Both within the staff and among board members, community organizations and individuals, and other libraries, the ability to work collaboratively is hardly a new skill in libraries but on that will be increasingly important . . ." The future of library business services rests on collaboration between librarians, communities, business organizations, and more.

It is so important for the success of your business center. In order to grow and succeed, you must leave the traditional boundaries of the library and build relationships with the local business community. Forming relationships takes much time and effort, but they are key to developing strategic partnerships that will allow for future growth.

Do your homework before reaching out to potential partners or collaborators. Potential partners should have an understanding of each other's organizational culture and mission before entering into the partnership. The first thing is to know what your mission is. If you don't have one, work with your director and colleagues to create one. Once you understand fully what you are trying to accomplish with your business services, you can express it to potential collaborators and partners.

Now you can look at different business organizations to see which would be the best fit for your library. A partnership allows its participants to draw on the resources and expertise of the partner organizations. These partnerships can exist on several levels depending on the goals and needs of the organizations. Consider your local chamber of commerce, SCORE, Small Business Administration, Small Business Development Center, Rotary, and more. Do your research so you understand the organization you are approaching. What are they offering that complements what you are doing? Are there some things both of you are doing? Can you work together to eliminate the overlap? Before contacting anyone, prepare ideas for potential ways you can work together.

All the business librarians we have spoken to over the last year have credited some part of their success, whether it be with a program or an event or research, to a local partner in the business community.

Sonya Durney, business specialist at PPL, told us about her first foray into the business community. Instead of being generalists, the reference librarians at PPL are specialists—each performs collection development, programming, outreach, and general reference services. The specialties are Business and Government, Health and Literacy, Science and Technology, and Cultural Subjects (music, art, history, etc.). The current Business and Government team leader, Sonya Durney, has a background in political science and was a restaurant manager for 20 years before coming to librarianship. Her first endeavor as the business specialist was to get out and meet local business organizations, specifically her local SCORE office. Sonya went to find out what the organization could do for the library's business patrons and was surprised to be asked "Why would I go to the library for business information?" When asked what PPL's mission for local business was, Sonya was not prepared with her elevator speech. However, she was not discouraged. Back to her library, she went where she spent some time solidifying what exactly the PPL was going to be offering its business patrons. This allowed her to determine what she needed in a business partner. Two months later, Sonya returned to SCOREMaine with an eloquent pitch detailing the library's mission to support local business and demonstrating the library's online business resources—hoping a partnership could happen. It worked and now SCOREMaine is one of the best advocates PPL has. Once a quarter, Sonya teaches a class about PPL's business resources with SCOREMaine.

Now Sonya's biggest focus is meeting people and advocating for the library. She spends a lot of time doing outreach, which includes going to local companies and business conferences and presenting. She is very active in local business activities, including Portland's first Startup Weekends, and she has been on the steering committee for Maine Start-up and Create Week Conference since its inception. Not only is she on the conference's steering committee, but she is also a speaker.

Joe Collier has been a business reference librarian at the Mount Prospect Public Library (MPPL) for three years. His predecessor had an ad hoc partnership with the local government and area chamber of commerce with no major programs or services. It wasn't until Joe participated in Synergy: The Illinois Library Leadership Initiative that he truly understood how to make that happen. The program helped him expand his vision of the library's business services. Focusing on community partnership, it asked how do you have influence and how can you use that to forge relationships. It showed Joe that it wasn't only the library director who had influence. He was attending many local business breakfasts and chamber of commerce events, often sitting next to the mayor or the city planner. Joe began to build relationships and was even on a first-name basis with them. He realized his one influence and how he could use it to grow business services at the library—ask them what the library can do to help them. From this question, an ad hoc relationship became a true and mutually beneficial partnership.

Mount Prospect Entrepreneurs Initiative (MPEI) is "not an incubator, not an institute," says Joe. MPEI is a "clearly focused business group" offering local businesses and entrepreneurs the tools they need for business success in Mount Prospect, Illinois. The tools include workshops, networking opportunities, an advisor's roundtable, and connections to successful entrepreneurs. Launched in fall 2015, the benefits to the library and its business services have been plentiful, including increased attendance at library business programs, elevated legitimacy of the library within the business community, and a grounding of the library in the community as a whole.

Formal and informal networks and partnerships are crucial to the success of your services and can promote the library's credibility as a regional resource for business information. If you want to be successful, you must be part of the community. And, additional revenue received through partnerships and networks broadens the selection of resources and services the library can make available to their local business patrons.

Getting Away from the Desk

Joe Collier and MPEI are perfect examples of getting away from the desk (See Figure 3.2). Joe attended some trainings and local business meetings

MOUNT PROSPECT
ENTREPRENEURS
INITIATIVE

RESOURCES TO ENCOURAGE, STRENGTHEN
AND SUPPORT SMALL BUSINESS

WWW.MOUNTPROSPECT.ORG/MPEI

 Educational Workshops
Licensing & Permit Guidance
Data Reference By Appointment
Available Property Listings

 Networking Opportunities
E-Newsletters & Social Media
Access to Advisors

 Promotion & Marketing
Entrepreneurship Recognition

Village of Mount Prospect
Mount Prospect Chamber of Commerce
Mount Prospect Public Library
Mount Prospect Downtown Merchants Association

Figure 3.2 An example of Mount Prospect Entrepreneurs Initiative's publicity material: simple and informative.

and made significant connections. Remember, it's not where your library is; it's where the small business owners are. An important way we offer services to businesses is to get into the business community. In order to make these connections, we must get out of the library. As a business librarian, you'll need to be comfortable networking with business owners. It's not easy, especially if you've never done it before. But it will be necessary for many reasons. Besides, sometimes there are refreshments; and who doesn't like appetizers and refreshments?

It's time for your first meeting/event. You pull up to a nondescript office building in the middle of an industrial park. First thing you notice is a number of folks strolling in with business folders and day planners. They look as thrilled as you do at eight in the morning. There's a small flutter in the pit of your stomach. You take one last sip of your coffee, because frankly you have no idea what to expect inside as far as "refreshments." Go to more than two of these, and you will realize it's a subjective term.

Upon entering what is usually a room too small (or too big) for the event, you quickly glance around at your fellow attendees and curse yourself under your breath that you didn't dress a certain way. Business casual? Suit, tie, skirt? Polo? You'll never know. You'll also notice that everyone has a name tag, which in many cases includes their name and company. This, you will later find out, will be the number one conversation starter for you: when Bob from A2 Marketing Inc. glances at your tag and sees "Library" or "Business Center," he will look at you puzzled and ask, "What exactly do you do?" Take a deep breath. Here comes the pitch.

You know what's great? What you are offering is free or low-cost. Your biggest challenge will be convincing the small business owner that there are no strings attached.

"So you have databases that will help me find manufacturers in Jefferson County that have a building size of 10,000 square feet or more? And it's in a spreadsheet? And it's free?"

Yes, we do. We've been hugged, kissed, and even patted on the head by patrons after we've delivered their data. It's a great feeling that we hope you get to experience some day. In the meantime, brush up on your sales pitch and get ready to hit the streets.

Take this exchange as an example:

Small Company CEO:	Hi Brad … [looks at your name tag] Williams Public Library … what do you do?
Super Hero Librarian:	I'm a business librarian at Williams Public Library.
Small Company CEO:	Business librarian? *Sounds interesting.*
Super Hero Librarian:	We provide business reference services to small businesses and entrepreneurs. If you are looking for demographics, industry information, or competitive lists, we can help you do that. You should really take advantage of it. It's really a great way to build your business, and it's completely free. No charge at all.
Small Company CEO:	*[head explodes]*

Remember that pitch!
According to Investopedia, an elevator pitch is "a slang term used to describe a brief speech that outlines an idea for a product, service or project. The name comes from the notion that the speech should be delivered in the short time period of an elevator ride, usually 20–60 seconds" (Investopedia 2017).

Perfecting this pitch is important to consider once you start getting out into the business community. Often you will only have a few moments to speak to each person you may meet. While you want to "sell" your services, the real key is to make them want to hear more. Not sure where to start with your pitch? Think about the best introductions you have heard from businesspeople and how you can tailor it to fit the library's services. Your pitch should make it clear why they should want to listen to you. Consider what you can offer them and give them a reason to contact you for a follow-up.

Check out sample elevator pitches online for some ideas—there are thousands. And practice, practice, practice. Your pitch should sound natural; it shouldn't sound rehearsed or rote.

Embedded Librarians

Recently, we have been hearing a lot about embedded librarians. Embedded librarians move out of the library and into the world they are looking to assist.

> Embedded librarianship is a distinctive innovation that moves the librarians out of libraries and creates a new model of library and information work. It emphasizes the importance of forming a strong working relationship between the librarian and a group or team of people who need the librarian's information expertise. As the relationship develops, the librarian's knowledge and understanding of the group's work and objectives grow, which leads in turn to greater alertness to the information and knowledge needs of the group. (Shumaker 2012, 4)

We suspect that many of you have been embedded librarians for many years just without the new name. More than just outreach, becoming embedded means you are truly in the community, forming relationships with that community. Business librarians are especially well versed in this as traditionally entrepreneurs and businesspeople haven't thought of the library as a resource that can work for them. The only way to get to entrepreneurs is to go to them. Also, working with businesses from multiple industries will sharpen your reference skills and increase awareness of business information needs.

Becoming an embedded librarian does not mean you need to have a physical space within a business or organization; it means that sometimes you are meeting them in their environment. Embedded business librarians attend gatherings and meetings of local business meetings—chambers of commerce, rotary clubs, networking groups, any organization or group that attracts entrepreneurs and businesspeople. Meetup.com has also become a good resource for grassroots entrepreneur groups.

Don't feel like you have to go to every single business function in your area. Attend as many as you can until you find the ones that work best for you and then become an active member. This is how you can reach people and make a difference. Once you have met people and formed some relationships, speak with someone about having some time at an upcoming meeting to discuss the business resources available at your library.

When you are given the opportunity, create a presentation that focuses on resources people might not realize are available through the local public library. Let them know you have databases that can give them insight into their competitors and customers. Tell them about the great social media programs you offer. Talk about how they can get a library card for their businesses. Most important is to give them a reason to connect with you again. Offer to give anyone a one-on-one or group tutorial on a specific database.

This is an important way to reach the businesses that need you the most. Take the Downtown Kings Mountain Small Business Success Project from the Mauney Memorial Library in North Carolina. Many new businesses in downtown Kings Mountain were opening and closing very quickly. Interviews with entrepreneurs were conducted to determine possible causes of the business failures. Results showed that the businesses lacked the fundamentals needed to start a business. These fundamentals included ignorance of using and accessing available resources. Library director, Sharon Stack, received a grant and created the Downtown Kings Mountain Small Business Success Project.

The most important aspect of the project was having an embedded business librarian, Heather Sanford, who would work very closely with these entrepreneurs at their businesses. Heather was out in the community from the beginning. She became very involved with the businesses that were part of the program. She went to them so they did not have to leave their businesses to come to the library. "The library follows me. I am the library," says Heather. Over two years, being embedded in the businesses enabled Heather to really understand what skills and resources they needed. This translated into help as simple as setting up an e-mail account using a smartphone to something as involved as creating a new brand for the business. Both Sharon and Heather agree that the impact of these relationships continues far past the end date of the project.

Coworking Space

We spoke about coworking spaces bit in Chapter 2, Setting Up Your Space, but would like to take a little more time to speak about it here. While many library business centers have been informal hubs of coworking among entrepreneurs and small business owners, the service has become more official recently. For many libraries throughout the country, offering coworking space has become an important part of their business services.

Coworking spaces give small businesses, perhaps with no formal office space outside of the home, a place to meet, collaborate, and create. For some, it is an opportunity to work in a new space and perhaps reenergize their workflow.

As with any library offering, *service is key*. While many of the same concepts hold true when working with your business population, some adjustments must be made for the audience. You must be committed to helping patrons who in many cases are wandering about into a new life without any direction. Be their beacon. Take the extra minute to ask more specific questions. Take the time to find out what they are hoping to accomplish in their new business endeavor. The more often you do so, the easier (and faster) you will become in getting your patrons not only what they want but also what they need.

Remember This

Your best work may be done outside of your library.

CHAPTER 4

Deep in the Data

So you are starting to get some solid business questions, and you know you are going to need to increase your resources. How do you start?

Most importantly, if patrons are asking you for the same thing over and over again, it might be time to consider getting a resource that can help you answer those questions, within reason. You most certainly do not want to break your budget because a patron asked a very detailed question about a very niche industry. There may be a resource to answer that very detailed question, and it may cost thousands of dollars per year. Do you really want to spend that much money when you suspect only this patron will ever need the information? Probably not. Do not fall into that trap of making one type of business owners happy in your community to leave the others to fend for themselves. There are plenty of "almost perfect" resources available. In many cases, almost perfect is better than nothing at all, especially when dealing with very expensive resources.

For example, we tend to get lots of questions dealing with specific industries—very *specific* industries. For example, it might be an up-and-comer such as an energy auditor. These are the folks who go into office buildings, retail, restaurants, and the like and let them know that if they change out their traditional light bulbs and replace them with energy-efficient ones, they can save such and such amount per month in energy costs.

You may get a request from one of them asking, "Is there a way you can tell me which businesses are using traditional light bulbs?" Ah, no. Or even better: "Can you tell me which businesses are already using an energy auditor?" Wish we could but, *nah*. But wait dear reader: there is hope for you and your patron. Do a little digging. Is there some sort of trade organization associated with energy auditors? Why? Yes, there is:

The Association of Energy Engineers. Perhaps they have data that could be beneficial. You'd be surprised how many trade organizations have data on their sites, and many times they are free. Additionally, a popular database that we will mention in this chapter, ReferenceUSA, offers users information on business expenses such as Utilities.

Now we've been doing this long enough to know these are the roads you go down when asked a question that may be a little "challenging." If you are just getting started, you may not travel down those roads yet, but with this book as your guide, we hope your trip will be a little less *bumpy*.

Here's another question we get a lot, especially from HR and employee benefits folk: "Is it possible to find out who is signed up for a 401k in their company?" These types of business owners would love to know which companies do not offer benefits so they can go in there and get a crack at them. Rightfully so, this information would be gold, except it is just not available. You'll get lots of requests for private information, and you'll most likely come up with a wonderfully diplomatic and kind response rather than "Are you kidding?"

Choosing Databases

We will keep saying this: selecting the databases that are right for you and your patrons is incredibly important. There are many different resources that do the same thing: some better than others, but in our research we found that there was no one "perfect" database. Luckily for us, there's a lot of competition out there between these companies, and every year you'll find a new feature added, or a tweak to their interface that edges one over the other.

When choosing which databases you will add to your collection, it is important to consider what types of business reference questions you are getting. There are a plethora of excellent databases available. Don't subscribe to a database because it's popular at other business libraries if it doesn't fit the needs of your library. You may be at a conference and hear over and over about a particular database. Maybe you stop at the company's booth, get a demonstration, and fall in love! *Look at the charts! Look at all the information!* Ask yourself, "What business reference questions am I currently getting that can be answered with this database?" If you can't think of three questions quickly, it may not be the database for your library.

Of course there are exceptions to this. Sometimes you may have to purchase a niche database to fulfill a need. For instance, the Miller Center subscribes to CoreLogic's RealQuest Professional, a property and property ownership database. We purchased this database after we began getting requests for commercial property owners as well as tax map information. After reviewing the database, we considered cost and usage. We were able to negotiate a small subscription—one user, in-house only, covering only our county—that worked for our patrons and, more importantly, our budget.

Our reviewed selections are most certainly not the only databases out there. We selected these databases based on our research, in which we surveyed over 100 librarians and asked them what they were using. Let this list be a starting point, not the be-all and end-all. After each database overview, we have included some sample reference questions that can be answered with the data.

AtoZ Databases

http://www.atozdatabases.com
DatabaseUSA
11211 John Galt Blvd.
Omaha, NE 68137
(877) 428-0101

Author's Rating	Price	Audience	Ease of Use	E-Mails?
****	$$$	Patrons, Librarians	Easy	Yes
Use it for: Creating marketing lists, getting e-mail contact information, company information.				
Bottom Line: Great database for beginners, very easy to use with lots of information.				

AtoZ does a lot of what some other databases do in this chapter (especially its brother from another mother ReferenceUSA), but one thing it has going for it is price and the ever-elusive availability of e-mail addresses. Patrons will be able to search based on company type, location, size, and a number of other useful criteria. The screen view for each company is well laid out and customizable, and it is here that users can browse the executive directory and e-mail addresses if available. Data can be downloaded into a spreadsheet, and the service offers an e-mailing feature of up to 500 e-mails per month through their partner. There's lots of competition out there, and clearly AtoZ is going after ReferenceUSA here. AtoZ has improved greatly from the time we first experienced it up to now, and there's a good chance they can equal and even overtake it. Only time (and new and improved features) will tell.

Following are sample questions where this database comes in handy:

> I'm looking to reach out to the human resource managers at all the local insurance companies. I really would like to e-mail them if possible.

> I'm a florist and business is so-so. I'm curious to see who my competitors are, where they are in relation to my shop, and how they are doing in terms of sales.

Business Source Premier

http://www.ebscohost.com/academic/business-source-premier
EBSCO Information Services
10 Estes Street
Ipswich, MA 01938
(800) 653-2726

Author's Rating	Price	Audience	Ease of Use	E-Mails?
*****	$$$	Patrons, Librarians	Easy	N/A
Use it for: Finding articles regarding a specific industry, product, or company; Download a report about a company.				
Bottom Line: Great resource for company reports and access to trade periodicals.				

One of the things Business Source Premier has going for it is scope: there are over 2,000 business periodicals available, plus all sorts of useful reports such as SWOT analysis, company profiles, and case studies. The user interface is clean and Google-like: enter a term in the search field and go. Much of what is available here is thankfully full text (good luck explaining to your patrons what an abstract is; sometimes they don't get it). We like to use this database for what we call "Corporate Intelligence": gathering info on a specific company, their competitors, and the industries. Results can sometimes be overwhelming and the interface hasn't changed much in the last few years, but the refinement tools and ease of downloading or printing articles put this database in our top three used.

Following are sample questions where this database comes in handy:

> I have a job interview at Canon USA, and I'd like to find out as much as possible about the company.

> I own an HVAC company and would like to find out what trends are happening in my industry.

Business Insights: Essentials

http://solutions.cengage.com/BusinessSolutions/Business-Insights-Essentials/
Gale Cengage
27500 Drake Road
Farmington Hills, MI 48331
(800) 877-4523

Author's Rating	Price	Audience	Ease of Use	E-Mails?
****	$$$	Patrons, Librarians	Easy	N/A
Use it for: Specific company information, market share data, and general industry information.				
Bottom Line: A wealth of information in an easy-to-use interface. We love this database for the market share reports.				

This tool for business owners, entrepreneurs, marketing professionals, investors, financial planners, and general researchers is easy to use and full of in-depth information on U.S. businesses and industries. If you are looking for a global spin, check out Business Insights: Global.

Following are sample questions where this database comes in handy:

> I need a history of the Costco Warehouse Corporation as well as a list of their competitors.

> How can I get a chart comparing sales at Target, WalMart, and Kmart?

Demographics Now

http://library.demographicsnow.com
Gale Cengage Learning
27500 Drake Road
Farmington Hills, MI 48331
(800) 877-4253

Author's Rating	Price	Audience	Ease of Use	E-Mails?
****	$$$	Patrons, Librarians	Easy	Yes
Use it for: Finding consumer spending trends; where business is being done based on geography; finding out how much your neighboring town spends on whiskey at home and peanut butter.				
Bottom Line: An easier way to access U.S. Census information.				

The data available through Demographics Now is downright fascinating. If you've ever tried getting demographics from the U.S. Census, you know it's a bit of a clunker of a database. Demographics Now takes all that data and presents it in a fairly easy-to-use interface. There are lots of bells and whistles available to the user, including a great mapping feature in addition to a fine collection of premade demographic reports. Ever wondered what the average household spends on whiskey or peanut butter? Health care? It's all here. And while we might not admit publicly that this is one of the resources that we geek-out about, we will certainly say it gets some of the best reactions out of our patrons during demonstrations.

Following are sample questions where this database comes in handy:

> I have the opportunity to purchase one of two existing pizzerias. One is in Lindenhurst, New York, and the other is in Middle Island, New York. Can you tell me which neighborhood would potentially have better sales?

> We are targeting consumers who are interested in children's clothing. We'd like to know which zip codes in central Florida spend the most.

D&B Million Dollar Database

http://www.mergentmddi.com
Mergent
580 Kingsley Park Drive
Fort Mill, SC 29715
(800) 342-5647

Author's Rating	Price	Audience	Ease of Use	E-Mails?
* * *	$$$	Patrons, Librarians	Moderately Easy	No
Use it for: Compiling lists of potential customers.				
Bottom Line: We are told the database is being phased out and that's a shame.				

D&B Million Dollar Database used to be the go-to, no-holds barred, most used champion of a database in our repertoire. Now it is dying a slow, sad, and painful death. Mergent, the company that now manages this database, has been letting it die in favor of its *new hotness*, Mergent Intellect. What we did like about the database was the format in which records could be downloaded. Patrons like to use marketing lists to set up mailings or to populate their own customer databases. D&B kept all the important data for each record on one sheet and one line. Mergent Intellect does not do that. While many libraries still have access to D&B, we expect it to be phased out by the time you are reading this.

Following are sample questions where this database comes in handy:

> I need a list of all the fish distributors in the Seattle area.

> I'd like to know how many barber shops there are in Chicago.

Foundation Directory

http://fconline.foundationcenter.org
Foundation Center
32 Old Slip, 24th Floor
New York, NY 10005
(212) 620-4230

Author's Rating	Price	Audience	Ease of Use	E-Mails?
****	$$$$	Patrons, Librarians	Moderate	No
Use it for: Finding who's giving out money for specific business types.				
Bottom Line: One-stop shop for grant information.				

A common question we get all the time: "Where can I find grant money for my business?" The short answer is there is no grant money available to start your for-profit business. However, if your patron is working in the not-for-profit arena or part of an industry that has government support, such as the "green initiative," this is the database to send him or her to. This directory will offer you the opportunity to search for grantors of funding based on location, subject, type, and time frame. You'll also be able to research the grantors themselves and see their grant histories, description of their company, and contact information. Patrons will not apply for grants directly from this database, but many records will provide the means of being forwarded to that information.

Following are sample questions where this database comes in handy:

> We are a not-for-profit who provides support services to families with autistic children and would like to see if there are any funding opportunities available in Connecticut.

> What types of grants does the Blandin Foundation offer?

LexisNexis Dossier

http://www.lexisnexis.com
LexisNexis
230 Park Avenue
Suite 7
New York City, NY 10017
(888) 285-3941

Author's Rating	Price	Audience	Ease of Use	E-Mails?
****	$$$	Patrons, Librarians	Easy	Yes
Use it for: Getting executive contact information for specific companies.				
Bottom Line: The simple fact that e-mail addresses are available in many of the records will make this database a popular choice with entrepreneurs.				

This database will satisfy many of the common questions asked by patrons, specifically when doing a targeted search of companies in a unique industry based on geography. The easy-to-use interface that's part of the advanced search feature allows the users to enter their criteria and then view or download a list of results. The highlight feature here is the availability of e-mail addresses of the primary contacts on each record, though we haven't had the time to confirm the validity of these e-mails, from what we can see they are legit. Patrons will also enjoy the ability to download batches of records in the thousands, something that other databases tend to limit. This database may be more useful for gathering deeper information on a specific company, but at the same time a good starting point to creating marketing lists of potential customers for small business owners looking to target specific types of companies.

Following are questions where this database comes in handy:

Can we get a list of manufacturers of computer boards in Kentucky?

What is the e-mail address of the CEO of Starbucks?

Mergent Intellect

http://www.mergentintellect.com
Mergent
580 Kingsley Park Drive
Fort Mill, SC 29715
(800) 342-5647

Author's Rating	Price	Audience	Ease of Use	E-Mails?
* * *	$$$$	Patrons, Librarians	Moderate	No

Use it for: Downloading potential customer lists; researching a specific company; getting up-to-date news stories regarding companies and industries.

Bottom Line: Still getting the bugs out but most certainly worth the time.

This database has the potential to be your top choice for company listings, but it's not quite there yet. Mergent took all the data from the Dun & Bradstreet Million Dollar Database and jazzed it up in what is a very nice-looking interface. Users select specific criteria, and based on their selections are given results in an attractive on-screen format. Click on a company and see tabs chock-full of data such as histories, executive roster, financials, and live links to current news. One excellent feature for publicly traded companies is a visualization of the company stock price superimposed over a timeline of news items and press releases. You will also be able to download beautifully formatted Hoover's company reports in PDF format, of which you may customize them to just return the information that is important to your research. The issue we have with the database is regarding the downloading of the data, specifically the format that is available. Most, if not all, patrons will want their data in spreadsheet format to include the basic company information, financials, and primary contact, all on one line. This latest version of Mergent does not do that. Instead, the database will return a spreadsheet with separate tabs for company address, financial information, and primary contact person. Having the data separated this way is counterintuitive to what your patrons will be looking for. Most of them will be using these data to create mailings, and the time necessary to combine the information is prohibitive.

To their credit, the folks at Mergent are incredibly receptive to our suggestions on how this database could be a home run, and while we're not software engineers, we are curious as to why having the primary information on one line is an issue. We are hopeful that a future update will make this feature available.

Following are questions where this database comes in handy:

How many vitamin manufacturing companies are there in the Los Angeles metropolitan area?

Can I get a list of all the facilities managers who work for companies with more than 50 employees in zip code 32830?

Plunkett Research

www.plunkettresearch.com
Plunkett Research, Ltd.
P.O. Drawer 541737
Houston, TX 77254
(713) 932-0000

Author's Rating	Price	Audience	Ease of Use	E-Mails?
**	$$$	Librarians	Easy	No
Use it for: Market research, industry trends, informative reports and videos.				
Bottom Line: Lots of useful information for marketers and the videos are a nice touch.				

Recently given a much-needed facelift, Plunkett Research contains a wealth of industry and market information as well as company profiles. Each industry also includes a video introduction by Mr. Plunkett himself, among other metrics such as industry associations, executive lists, statistics, market trends, and industry-specific glossaries.

Following are questions where this database comes in handy:

What's the median home construction cost in the United States?

How many consumers play fantasy sports?

Redbooks Library Edition

http://www.redbooks.com
Redbooks
330 Seventh Avenue, Floor 10
New York, NY 10001
Phone: 800-908-5395

Author's Rating	Price	Audience	Ease of Use	E-Mails?
****	$$$	Librarians, Patrons	Easy	Yes
Bottom Line: Not just an advertising agency database: valuable information for budding marketers or business owners looking to get into creative design, advertising, and branding.				

How much money does Southwest Airlines spend on advertising on the radio? Who owns the OmniVision brand? Who is responsible for that annoying Target ad you saw last night? All these questions are answered and much more in the Redbook Library Edition database. Besides a comprehensive list of advertising agencies and companies who use them, you'll get financial information, a company's competitors, brand information, and e-mail addresses of key employees. Additionally, users can use powerful filters such as industry type, company size, revenue, and more. Browsing the Opportunities section, you can view articles on companies that are in the process of changing agency accounts. Your patron's business idea not panning out? Have them check out Redbook's Job Directory. Overall, this database would be a great addition to your collection, especially for those patrons who are looking to work in the creative and advertising fields.

Following are questions where this database comes in handy:

I just graduated from college with a marketing degree. Where can I find a job with an agency?

That new Target commercial is annoying. Who was responsible for that?

ReferenceUSA

http://www.referenceusa.com
Infogroup, Inc.
1020 E. 1st Street
Papillion, NE 68046
(800) 808-1113

Author's Rating	Price	Audience	Ease of Use	E-Mails?
*****	$$$	Patrons, Librarians	Easy	For Purchase
Use it for: Downloading lists of potential customers.				
Bottom Line: If you have the budget for *just one* database, this is it.				

If asked, "Which database should no business research collection be without?" it's ReferenceUSA. Very easy to use, providing easy-to-download results, ReferenceUSA will allow you and your patrons the ability to download lists of companies based on specific criteria. Looking for insurance brokers in Orlando, Florida, who have revenue over $500,000 and more than two employees? Select your criteria and click "View Results" and there you have it. Recently undergoing a bit of a facelift as well as a noticeable improvement in speed, we can confidently say that ReferenceUSA is a must for any business librarian and was rated as the most popular during our research survey.

Following are sample questions where this database comes in handy:

I'd like a list of all the law offices in Orange County who have 10 or more employees and have an annual revenue of over $10 million.

Can you get me a list of pet lovers in Santa Clara who make $75,000 or more in annual household income?

Simmons OneView

http://oneview.experian.com
Experian
475 Anton Blvd.
Costa Mesa, CA 92626
(866) 256-4468

Author's Rating	Price	Audience	Ease of Use	E-Mails?
* * *	$$$$	Librarians	Difficult	No
Use it for: Marketing, advertising, and consumer behavior research.				
Bottom Line: Great marketing data with unbelievable combinations but may take time to learn to use.				

The OneView database compiles fascinating consumer information such as purchasing habits and interests. The interface is somewhat cluttered and at first glance can be discouraging, but after getting to know the lay of the land and understanding the concepts of creating columns and drag-and-dropping metrics, it's a little easier to grasp. Want to know if 18–24-year-olds prefer Coca-Cola or Pepsi AND if they use social networks? This is your database.

Following are sample questions where this database comes in handy:

I need to know what percentage of men watch sports and are interested in exercise in the southwestern United States.

Which age group watches TV more often?

Small Business Resource Center

http://solutions.cengage.com/BusinessSolutions/Resource-Center/
Gale Cengage
27500 Drake Road
Farmington Hills, MI 48331
(800) 877-4523

Author's Rating	Price	Audience	Ease of Use	E-Mails?
****	$$$	Patrons, Librarians	Easy	N/A
Use it for: Finding real-life business plans.				
Bottom Line: Great resource for comprehensive business planning, including real-life business plan samples.				

With its recent redesign, Gale has made Small Business Resource Center even more valuable for budding entrepreneurs. The home page breaks the database up into its four major components and the same topics of most interest to entrepreneurs—Plan, Fund, Start, and Manage. Each section includes information from more than 80 business e-books, 300 journals, and thousands of business directory listings. For many, the most valuable part of the Small Business Resource Center are its 700+ real-life business plans. Business plans run the gamut from coffee shops to scrap metal salvage. In my own reference experience, I have always been able to find a plan that helps out a patron struggling on his or her own.

Following is a sample question where this database comes in handy:

> I need a business plan for my website development company before a banker will even meet with me.

Statista

http://www.statista.com
Statista, Inc.
55 Broad Street, 30th floor
New York, NY 10004
(212) 433-2270

Author's Rating	Price	Audience	Ease of Use	E-Mails?
★ ★ ★	$$$$	Librarians	Easy	No
Use it for: Industry trends, marketing information, pretty graphs and charts.				
Bottom Line: Expensive but easy to use with great-looking graphics and charts.				

Chock-full of statistics from Agriculture to Travel and Tourism, Statista is a trove of graphs, reports, and infographics (See Figure 4.1) that should satisfy anyone looking for hard data in an easy-to-digest format. The database is easy to use: search for a topic and see a listing of relevant results. Users can also browse through industries, topics, infographics, and digital markets. Statista is unfortunately one of the more expensive databases out there, mostly catering to big academic organizations. While the data here are most certainly useful, you'll have to weigh it against other, clunkier databases that may have the same data but do not present it as nicely as Statista (and at a lower price).

Following are sample questions where this database comes in handy:

> I'm doing a report about my herb-growing business and need some statistics and charts for my presentation.
>
> What do most people do when they browse the Internet?

As we mentioned at the beginning of this chapter, these are just a selection of the most popular business databases available. Consider carefully before choosing which databases to add to your collection. Many of the database publishers post lists of libraries that subscribe. Talk to a few of them, and gather their feedback. Speak to the sales rep, and request a webinar or meeting detailing what the database offers. Ask for a free trial, and use it to answer some frequent business questions you receive. Encourage your colleagues (whether they are business specialists or not) to try out the database. Is it easy to use? Does it have information you need? Can you get the information from another reputable source for less money? Some librarians get feedback from patrons before making a final decision. We suggest that you only involve patrons if there is a good chance you will be adding the database to your collection. You would hate

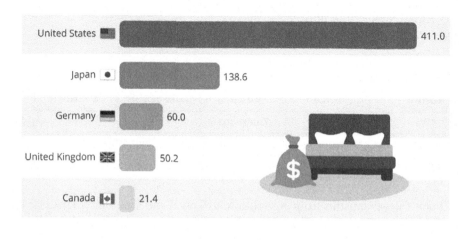

The Enormous Cost Of Sleep Deprivation

Estimated annual cost of insufficient sleep in GDP terms (billion U.S. dollars)*

- United States — 411.0
- Japan — 138.6
- Germany — 60.0
- United Kingdom — 50.2
- Canada — 21.4

statista

Figure 4.1 A typical Statista chart.

to show a business patron a phenomenal database that is so cost prohibitive that it has no chance of being added.

Once you have decided on a database, be sure to speak to the sales rep about different options. Is it available remotely or only to users in the library? Can you get a discount if you sign a multiyear contract? Databases are an important part of your services, and decisions pertaining to them should not be taken lightly.

Remember This

Databases can be expensive! Don't sign any contracts without much consideration on their potential use and value to your business community.

CHAPTER 5

Some of the Best Things in Life...

Wouldn't it be swell if the director handed you the library's credit card and said, "Here ... get what we need, and get what you want, too ..." For most, it's a dream. If you DO have that type of budget, make sure to check out Chapter 4, Deep in the Data, for some of our favorite subscription databases and go nuts.

You may or may not be surprised to know that there are many, many free resources available from your local government and local business organizations. We would even go so far to say that most likely there is a plethora of resources. Your town or county clerk's office will most likely give you public access to business data, especially information on new business formation. Looking for real estate information? Reach out to your local building or planning departments. You'll also want to connect with any business group that might meet in your immediate area. Many of them will offer membership directories for free; most of your local chambers will break down business types into categories. Simply doing a search for your local chamber of commerce's website should yield some results.

Remember to tap into your local news as well: local business papers or the business section of your local/regional paper will have news about your local economy, new business developments, local business laws, and in some cases, free access to data.

You should browse your local paper's business section on a regular basis. In some cases, they will cite data sources that are free and provided by the government. You'll also want to take a look at any relevant periodicals in your collection (and if they are not in your collection, you might want to consider adding them) for a mention of data resources.

Many states have dedicated resources for small businesses. In New York, we use the state's business site—http://www.ny.gov/services/business—or Empire State Development's www.NYlovesBiz.org to access basic business information and state-specific business programs. Starting at your state's home page and working from there is a great way to start building your valuable collection of free business sources. Or visit the federal government's BusinessUSA website—https:/business.usa.gov/micro-site/ state-resource—and start your search for state and local business resources.

Finally, let's emphasize the importance of having a relationship with your state's small business development organization: these folks are business counselors and are constantly dealing with data, metrics, and demographics. They may know something you don't, and vice versa.

The free resources highlighted here are not the only ones available out there. Some will be incredibly relevant to you and your patrons, and others will not be. We've selected these based on our experiences and our successes with helping our patrons find data using them.

Have a website?

Include a list of your favorite free online resources for your patrons to access. Market it accordingly. Make sure patrons know they are free and can be accessed from anywhere. Categorizing them by subject will be very helpful.

Company Information

Kompass—http://us.kompass.com/

The free component of this resource will give you the basics about a company or industry. The really great feature is being able to cross-reference other companies within the same industry of the one that you are viewing. Even better: looking for a company that supplies a certain part or chemical to other companies? You can use the supplier search feature to find them. You will not get the depth from this database that you would from subscription databases like Mergent or ReferenceUSA, but it's a great start. And of course, you can always upgrade your Kompass and pay for their subscription service to see all their data.

Manta—http://www.manta.com/

Manta is a database that is geared toward small business owners, primarily as a marketing tool. Businesses can register themselves on the database, and based on their application, they will be filed with other like businesses. Again, the free version will have limited information, but the ability to search based on location and business type can be helpful.

Demographics

American FactFinder—http://factfinder2.census.gov/faces/nav/jsf/pages/index.xhtml

Accessing any data from the U.S. Census can be a daunting task. There is a treasure trove of information here, but the challenge is navigating through it all. If you visited the site five years ago, you would have probably given up your search after a few minutes; but after a recent redesign and with the addition of a guided search feature, the information is a little easier to get to. Many budding entrepreneurs will ask you for demographic information, and this would be the place to come for it. The site includes data from the Annual Economic Surveys, Economic Census, and one of our favorites, the American Community Survey, which includes business patterns, business expenses, and industry trends. We won't admit that we come to this database on a Sunday afternoon, sipping a nice glass of chardonnay and pouring over things such as Commuting Characteristics by Sex or County Business Patterns. Sounds interesting, though.

American Time Use Survey—http://www.bls.gov/tus/

How much time does the average American spend working? Eating? Sleeping? Or what about playing sports? That small business owner who's looking to offer a new backyard lawn game might want to know, and this is the place to go. A great collection of tables and charts from the Bureau of Labor Statistics, this database also includes time spent on such mundane things as housework.

Consumer Expenditure Survey—https:/www.bls.gov/cex/

Wondering how much Americans are spending on gas? Or household items? Or any number of things? While certainly not the easiest way to get consumer expenditure information, the Bureau of Labor Statistics' Consumer Expenditure Survey is the direct source for the most up-to-date figures on consumer spending, income, and demographics.

DataUSA—http://datausa.io/

This downright beautiful website takes data from various sources and gorgeously illustrates it for consumption. Your eyes will delight in photos, charts, graphs, and fantastic demographic information. This will come in handy for small business owners looking to break into a particular industry or location.

Economic Census—http://www.census.gov/econ/census/
Business plans required lots of economic demographic information, and this is the place to get it. As of this writing, the U.S. Census was in the process of releasing data from the 2012 Economic Census. While navigating the site may induce migraines, ultimately you will come across excellent and useful information.

Pew Internet & American Life Project—http://pewinternet.org/
For information geeks like us, Pew Research Center's reports provide a fascinating look inside such topics as Social Media, Crowdsourcing, Internet Use, and more. Reports, datasets, and presentations can be downloaded in PDF format. We also highly recommend that you sign up for their newsletter, as you will be notified of new reports along with whatever other juicy information they are sharing that week. We also like saying their name: Pew. *Pew pew pew.*

Funding

CrunchBase—https://www.crunchbase.com/#/home/index
This is a great resource for anyone looking to research venture capitalists, angel investors, and business incubators. The database allows you to search for specific companies, investors, and products. Want to know who's invested in Nest Labs, the makers of home automation products? A search on this database will not only yield who invested, but in many cases, how much they invested. A brief bio or company history is usually included as well as live links to news, social networking channels, and employee roster. This database comes in handy especially for those techie entrepreneurs who have a great new idea and want to see who's investing in those ideas.

Grants.gov—http://www.grants.gov/
Small business owners are always looking for money, and while the majority of them wouldn't be eligible for a federal grant, this would be your go-to for those folks looking for funding based on a specific subject or need. It also includes a handy service called "Workspace" that will allow the patrons to create a single application for reuse as well as collaborate with other members of their staff in applying for a grant. While not a replacement, this is a decent alternative to the Foundation Directory.

Industry Information

North American Industry Classification System—http://www.census.gov/eos/www/naics/
You've probably guessed that we've committed all the North American Industry Classification System (NAICS) codes to memory, but if your patrons need to look them up, this is a great tool. The real benefit here is

being able to search based on keywords. What is practical about this database are the sector descriptions, which provide a brief description of the code and links to subcodes. We find that sometimes browsing these codes is a bit of an inspiration and will lead you down a more concise path to the companies you or your patrons are searching for.

Standard Industry Classification System—https:/www.osha.gov/pls/ imis/sicsearch.html
Did you know that the Standard Industry Classification (SIC) code was supposed to be replaced by NAICS in 1997? We wonder how that's going. Like the NAICS database, the SIC search tool will allow you to search based on SIC code or keyword. Clicking on a result will display both the industry group and all the subgroups as well.

ThomasNet—http://www.thomasnet.com/
ThomasNet is the massive manufacturer database, formerly known as the Thomas Register of American Manufacturers. Here users can search for products and suppliers through their easy-to-use search feature. Is your entrepreneur looking for a specific part for his or her invention? Maybe a bracket or button? Electronic components? Lubricants? This is the place to come. You'll even be able to view product catalogs from manufacturers around the country, and links to their websites make it easy to place an order.

Investing

Investopedia—www.investopedia.com
Investopedia's tagline, "Sharper Insight. Smarter Investing," accurately describes the content of this helpful website. Newbie business librarians and investors will find a plethora of information on wealth, finance, and investing. Most useful for these librarians has been the Investopedia Dictionary, covering in just enough detail many unfamiliar terms.

The Investor's Clearinghouse—http://www.investoreducation.org/
Supported by Alliance of Investor Education, Investor Education offers many detailed, yet easy-to-understand introductory guides covering bonds, options, mutual funds, and general investing.

Securities and Exchange Commission—www.sec.gov
The Securities and Exchange Commission's (SEC) mission is to protect investors. To that end they collect copious amounts of data on private for-profit companies. Use EDGAR to search more than 20 million filings for specific companies. The education portion of the website also offers guidance for investors with many tools for them, including how to choose a broker and how to calculate the costs of mutual funds.

Marketing

Marketing Charts—http://www.marketingcharts.com/
Who doesn't like charts, right? And these are pretty sweet: marketing folks should find the mostly free charts handy. Updated daily, users have access to consumer trends, spending behavior, and industry information. Another bonus: Marketing Reports, many of which are free, can be downloaded in handy PDF format. Best of all: if your patrons require a marketing chart for a report or business plan, they can use them as long as there is attribution to Marketing Charts.

GlobalEdge—http://globaledge.msu.edu/
GlobalEdge is a great source of international business information. Specifically, users can access something called the Market Potential Index, which ranks countries' markets allowing business owners to see the potential of being successful there.

KnowThis—http://www.knowthis.com/
A simple collection of links to marketing articles, tutorials, and research resources for those patrons looking to market their business.

Patents, Trademarks, and More

Google Advanced Patent Search—http://www.google.com/advanced_patent_search
Do you use Google to search the Internet? Of course you do. So this should seem familiar and easy to use for you. What's nice about this resource is your ability to search across multiple criteria, including date and classification. It's also much, much easier to navigate, and search this resource than the U.S. Patent Office's database.

Patent and Trademark Office—http://www.uspto.gov/
While Google Patent Search is an easy way to search patents, the Patent and Trademark Office site is a great resource for everything else: the patent process overview, fee information, and policy information. Also available here and not at Google is the trademark database. Not as easy to search as Google but certainly after spending a few minutes poking around, you and your patrons should be able to find their next big thing. Be sure to also utilize the resources at your local Patent and Trademark Resource Center (PTRC). Specialists are available for assistance. Locations of all the PTRCs can be found at https:/www.uspto.gov/learning-and-resources/support-centers/patent-and-trademark-resource-centers-ptrcs.

Small Business Support

BPlans—www.bplans.com
Although a gateway to paid content, there is enough valuable, free content on BPlans to include it on this list of free resources. Each of the over 500 free business plans is robust and includes company summary, market analysis, management summary, and a financial plan. Online calculators help entrepreneurs calculate break-even, starting costs, and cash flow.

Business Plans—http://www.referenceforbusiness.com/business-plans/
Every new business should start with a business plan, but entrepreneurs often don't know where to start. Seeing a business plan from a similar business often starts the gears working toward their own plan. This site offers free access to much of the content of Gale Cengage's multivolume *Business Plans Handbook.*

Mission Statements—http://www.missionstatements.com/company_mission_statements.html
This database highlights both the realistic, and sometimes lofty, mission statements of the world's largest and most successful companies. It also serves as a marketing platform for the company that writes mission statements, but there's a ton of inspiration here that will be both useful and inspirational to the budding entrepreneur.

New York State Business Services—http://www.ny.gov/services/business
This is an example of a state-specific general website. As we mentioned earlier in the chapter, these types of websites are important to include on your list of resources. They are helpful for your business patrons and invaluable to business librarians. Check out BusinessUSA to start the search for your state and local resources.

Small Business Administration—https://www.sba.gov/
This website is the fledgling small business owner's one-stop shop to everything from the government's Small Business Administration (SBA). Broken down neatly into sections, you should encourage your patrons to visit here first, especially if they are in the early stages of starting their business. This is the portal to the SBA loan application process, and as we've already mentioned, entrepreneurs will most likely ask you where they can get money for their business. This is one option. We also like the SBA's Learning Center, a collection of free online courses with subjects ranging from customer service to writing a business plan to cybersecurity.

SBDC Clearinghouse—http://www.sbdcnet.org/
A treasure trove of free market research reports, industry information, articles on small business, and "client stories," this database also includes links to many other resources (mostly government, mostly free) that we've already mentioned here and some we have not. You would be doing a disservice to your patrons if you do not include this site as a resource on your web page.

Statistics

BizStats—www.bizstats.com
While not the prettiest of sites, it does include valuable insights, including business financial ratios for 250 industries and other business and industry statistics.

Bureau of Labor Statistics—http://www.bls.gov/
Small business owners might not be interested in the unemployment rate or information on careers, but they will be interested in such things as labor productivity and costs, average per hour salaries in their county, and employment costs, especially when hiring their work force. Is it super easy to get what you're looking for? Not quite, but it is free and the data go deep. Most importantly, any business owner who has employees needs to know information such as benefits, productivity, and safety.

BusinessUSA—https:/business.usa.gov/
This one-stop platform was created by the federal government to "quickly connect businesses to the services and information relevant to them, regardless of where the information is located." Its aim is to cut through the bureaucracy many small business and entrepreneurs face when looking for government information. According to its About page, "BusinessUSA is your front door to all the government has to offer" (https:/business.usa.gov/about-us). The front page breaks out the most-needed information with headings like Grow Your Business, Explore Government Contracting, and Learn about Taxes and Credits, making it a very helpful resource.

ZanRan Numerical Data Search—http://www.zanran.com/q/
While still in beta, ZanRan is a neat, little search engine that crawls the Internet for documents that contain data and statistics using a brilliant algorithm created by two fellows from England. If the document is found, it is indexed and accessible for all to see. Do a search for Export to China and you'll get thousands of results with graphs and charts. While not the most elegant of interfaces, in the end this is lots of useful data and it is all free for the taking.

There are so many great free resources out there to help you and your patrons with business research. This chapter is a great start, but you should be updating and adding to your list all the time.

Remember This

You don't need a cache of expensive databases to help businesses and entrepreneurs.

CHAPTER 6

Old School: A Quick Note on Print

While this book is firmly planted in the digital world, we feel it necessary to take a small step back for a moment and talk about some old school resources that are worthy of your attention. Frankly, if you've been given the OK by your administration to have a few shelves worth of business books, why not fill them with things that your patrons might pick up and flip through or even, dare we say, check out for 21 days?

When considering what to order, revisit the ways we discussed becoming a better business librarian—read classic business titles, keep up-to-date with business newspapers and periodicals, and talk to businesspeople. These ideas can also be used to decide what books to include in your collection. The specific business titles and authors we wrote about in previous chapters are a great start to your circulating business collection. Other business libraries can guide you in collection development; find libraries that are similar to yours in location and size and browse their shelves—virtually or in-person. Business-specific publishers, like those listed next, will also get you started.

Amacom Books

Broadway Business

Crown Business

Entrepreneur Press

FT Press

Harvard Business Publishing

McGraw-Hill Professional

Nolo

Business and nonfiction best-seller lists are your collection development friends, especially when you are just starting out. These are a true window into what books entrepreneurs and businesspeople are buying—whether they read them or not, we'll never know. At the Miller Center, we visit the *Wall Street Journal* business best-seller list, and we have *every book* on the list in our collection. Once you start looking, you will notice many of the titles are perpetually on the list. Consider these books and their authors. Do they have other titles? Do you own them? What books do they recommend?

We mentioned this before and must mention it again: read *Entrepreneur* magazine and *Inc.* and any other business magazines accessible to you. Your collection-building skills can truly be honed by flipping through these publications. Not only will you potentially get reviews of new business books, but you'll also be able to see what people are talking about, what trends are taking place, and where you need to be.

Out of the University of Florida, Business Books: Core Collections (http://businesslibrary.uflib.ufl.edu/businessbooks) is a plethora of invaluable collection development information. Developed and maintained by business librarian, Peter Z. McKay, it is a carefully curated collection covering major business topics such as accounting, consumer behavior, and leadership. Each individual book selection includes cover art and a summary. Business Books: Core Collections is a great resource for all business librarians, especially those who are building a new collection.

Currently in its fifth edition, *The Basic Business Library: Core Resources and Services* is a must-have for any business librarian, especially the newbies. In the past, a large portion of the book covered core print resources. While not as relevant in this digital age, the new edition does touch upon valuable print resources and even discusses out-of-print titles.

Business periodicals should also be a consideration when planning your print collection. While many will be available in your databases, offering browsing copies will appeal to those entrepreneurs and businesspeople visiting business library. At the Miller Center, the most popular periodicals in our browsing collection are *Entrepreneur, Investor's Business Daily, Harvard Business Review,* and *The Chief,* a New York-based newspaper focused on local government and civil service employees.

Reference books are a whole other ball game. These are usually "big-ticket" expensive items that will require much contemplation on whether or not they are worthy of being part of your print collection.

Another aspect of building your print reference collection that you need to consider is audience. You will most certainly have patrons with varying degrees of knowledge, reading ability, and computer skills. We certainly do not want to disparage any of our patrons, but let's be candid: some folks will not want to sit down at a computer and dig through a database for information. Even in this day and age, we are still far from a time where books are obsolete, everyone has a smartphone in their pocket, and the Internet can be navigated with the greatest of ease.

Visit any of the up-and-coming business centers throughout the country, and besides a bank of computers with business databases, you'll see someone sitting at a table, with pen or pencil in hand, scribbling furiously on a notepad, and open books. We don't know about you, but for us, there is something that is still important—something *reassuring*—with the tactile experience of flipping through a reference book and moving your fingers up and down a page. The smell of a newly printed book is something special, isn't it? When it comes to replacing this feeling with something similar in digital form, we haven't quite got there yet. While our primary focus on resources in this book has been digital, there are still plenty of patrons looking to start a business who want to grab something off the shelf and either bring it home or sit down at a table and dig into it.

Sometimes it is simply a matter of appearances. We don't expect you to go out and order the full 30-volume set of your state's laws along with the huge collection of *Supreme Court Reporter*. But what a nice display it makes! It looks sharp, and it's a great background for important pictures. But in all seriousness, while many, if not all, of the laws of your state and our federal government are available online, some patrons will be more comfortable flipping through a big ol' book. Legal collections are where many people are putting their print budgets. In our experience, the layperson is much more confortable browsing a law book than wading through different cases on a legal database.

Thomson Reuters (http://legalsolutions.thomsonreuters.com/) has a wide array of legal reference books and volumes that range in price from $60 up to thousands of dollars. It's worth taking a look at what they offer for your local community or region. While much of what is offered in print is available via their electronic resources, Westlaw being the standard for case law research, you'll need to do a cost-benefit analysis on your print and digital options when it comes to law books. Most entrepreneurs will be interested in business law, so focus on those titles first and then build out from there.

More affordable and geared toward the do-it-yourself crowd, Nolo (www.nolo.com) is a fantastic resource for books on finance, legal forms, incorporation information, real estate, employer/employee issues, and more. Besides publications, their website includes a great lawyer search engine that will allow your patrons to search for and find local lawyers who focus on all manner of legal issues, from Product Liability and Intellectual Property to Workers Compensation and Commercial Real Estate.

Business reference books are generally very expensive. Do your research when building your print collection: you might be able to not only secure the print copies but also access to databases as well. Many publishers will offer either e-book access or, in some cases, access to the raw data that are included in the publication. Gale/Cengage (www.cengage.com) is a great example of this. Their business resources and encyclopedias are available in print and e-book format, and their business databases pull data from their print collections. Build relationships with your sales reps. Don't be afraid to ask for deals or ask for packages that include both print and digital. There's a lot of competition out there, and there is always room for haggling. Some publishers may also offer first-time discounts, so be sure to mention that as well.

It's important to have a nice mix of both print and digital in your collection. If you are lucky enough to be given a budget, take that magic number and try a few different combinations of material types. You are just getting started; there's no need to get absolutely everything. You also may find that certain industries are so niche that having a database rather than a book on the shelf doesn't make sense. Take, for example, the construction industry. On Long Island, we have a number of small business owners who are contractors. Many of them come in to use the RSMeans Construction Cost Data books (www.rsmeans.com) that we have in our print collection. While available electronically, we decided that it didn't make sense to spend the money on the digital version when the majority of the patrons using this resource did not want it electronically. They want to come in, pull the book off the shelf, find the report they are looking for, either copy the page or transcribe it into their little black book, and be on their way. The same holds true for the Long Island Construction Bulletin from CMD Group, a weekly newsletter of current local construction jobs out for bid. Even if we were able to purchase it as a database, we probably wouldn't switch over.

Your physical space may also dictate how many and what types of print resources you will be offering, so keep this in mind as well. Regardless, although we are living in the digital age, the printed book still lives on. A thoughtful plan taking into account what type of patrons you have, what types of information they are looking for, and the importance of having a well-rounded collection that includes both print and digital resources is the best approach.

Remember This

Even in the digital age, we still want physical books.

CHAPTER 7

Programming and Special Events

While space, collections, and research assistance are important components for business services, programming should not be forgotten. Programming is a key component to the success of any public library, and it is also integral to a library's business services. Programming can enable you to attract an even more diverse group of businesspeople. Many of you are familiar with programming for the general public. Although similar, programming for the business community presents different challenges. They are often pulled in many directions at work and by other business organizations and will only choose programs/meetings/events that they see as a good use of their time.

Offering programs that appeal to your business population gives educational opportunities that might not be available to them. Keep in mind that many entrepreneurs still need the basics. "Anyone can have a good idea for a product or service—but many lack core competencies for full participation in today's economy" (ALA 2016). Sure they might not sound too exciting, but a program covering the basics of a business plan might be your most popular and needed program. Many entrepreneurs start a business based on need or opportunity and then educate themselves.

We've mentioned networking and will continue to as it is that important. Networking with other entrepreneurs and businesspeople is key to business success. Programming is an opportunity for them to do this. It gets businesspeople out from behind their desks or stores and around other businesspeople. Many entrepreneurs work solo and may spend a lot of time alone. Programming with built-in networking offers them a connection to other entrepreneurs they might not be getting on a day-to-day basis. Sometimes the educational component is just an extra added value and incentive.

Starting a new programming effort isn't difficult, but it does take time and thought. You are getting out there; you are helping business patrons. What do they need? What questions are they asking? What are they talking about? What topics are in high demand? Think about the specific questions you are getting. Do business patrons ask about finding new customers? Do they wonder about setting up a Facebook page for their business? Are they asking how they can patent a new invention? Is there a very popular business book heavily circulating right now?

Before you finalize your program topics, determine when you will offer your programs. As with all programming, it is important to consider your audience when setting program times, days, and duration. What are other local business organizations doing? Are their programs in the evening? Have you noticed that most business events you have attended are in the morning? How long are the events?

Some libraries do well with programs on Saturdays or the evenings, while others have found that their family-oriented business patrons are looking for early morning programs. They want to start the day early and be home in the evening and on weekends. Ask people what works best. Try a variety of different times/days of the week, and see which gets the best attendance and feedback. Also keep in mind meeting times and dates of local business organizations. If you know the local chamber of commerce meets every Thursday at 9:00 a.m., you should avoid programming at that time. Determining the best days/times will come with trial and error. Most important to remember is that you may have to offer many programs many times before you find out what works best for your community.

Just like you consider the program when setting up the space for your general population, you must carefully consider the space for business programs. As we mentioned, business programming not only gives patrons an opportunity to learn, it also gives them an opportunity to meet other business owners and entrepreneurs. Use your programs to facilitate these connections because they are so important to the success of any businessperson. Offer name tags for attendees to fill out. Andy Woodworth, from Cherry Hill Public Library, creates name badges based on a program's registration list.

Another easy way to do is accomplished merely through setting up a space that is conducive to discussion. How is that done? If you have enough space, say no to audience-style seating. Rather than just having rows of chairs facing a speaker, arrange the space so it encourages discussion. Set up small tables and chairs, ideally with four people

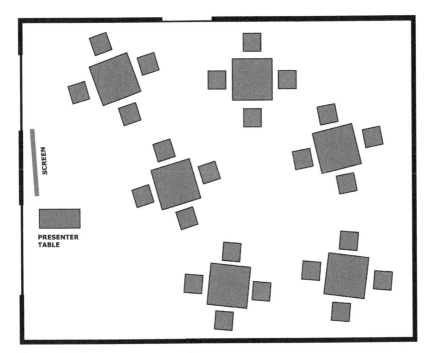

Figure 7.1 Room set-up example.

per table (See Figure 7.1). The tables give attendees a place for their beverages and an easy way to take notes. It also forces people to introduce themselves and find out about the other person's business. It makes them talk with each other. It's a win-win for all parties. To increase these opportunities, schedule networking times into your program times. Your program starts at 10 a.m.? Open the doors at 9:30 a.m. and encourage attendees to arrive early to meet each other.

Want to take it a step further? At a recent business program, Andy Woodworth of Cherry Hill Public Library, New Jersey, required all attendees to preregister. When they arrived, preprinted name badges were waiting for them. Name badges can help alleviate the stress involved with meeting new people and can especially help if you've forgotten the name of someone you met at the last library program you attended.

While it is not always possible due to budget constraints, offering coffee/tea or other refreshments before a program is a great way to get attendees in early. Generally speaking, coffee/tea is inexpensive. Approach your director. If he or she has supported your move toward the business community, he or she will have an open ear to your suggestions. If the money is just not available, consider visiting a local coffee shop or supermarket (something you should be doing anyway!) and asking for a donation for the program or program series. In turn, offer to put their company information on the marketing materials or next to the refreshments at the program.

OK, so you have some possible dates and times. You've spoken with many businesspeople and have a handle on different topics they are thinking about. Now it is time to turn those questions and concerns into programs!

Aspiring and new entrepreneurs need lots of help, guidance, and mentoring. Because of this, programs targeted to their needs are generally very popular. A series of programs on starting a business can help these entrepreneurs learn about regulatory requirements, start-up loans, business plans, basic marketing, and more. Potential program topics could be as basic as How to Start Your Own Business or Small Business Finances. New entrepreneurs and established businesspeople are always interested in growing their businesses. No matter the economy, programs on marketing and gaining new business are worthwhile.

You can also bring in the actual businesspeople your center helped. Success stories are great for you, your library, and your business patrons. A patron with a successful business sharing his or her story can be a great motivator for other patrons starting a business.

So you've got some ideas. You've got a space ready to go. And the local coffee place said they'd donate some refreshments. Who's going to present all these programs? Think of your ideas. Think of what you've decided your business community is hungry for. Now decide which of those topics are in line with your knowledge and experience. As a librarian you have probably presented a program at some point in your career. Maybe you are an armchair genealogist or a knitter or an expert at downloading e-books—all of these skills can translate into wonderful introductory programs for your patrons. Why not use your skills for the business community as well? Lead a business book discussion; give an introductory class on Facebook; show people how to make a table in Microsoft Word; demonstrate a business database; or lead a panel discussion. An ideal program for every library business center is an introduction to the library services you offer local businesses. This type of program is a great way to meet your audience and market your services. It also introduces you (and your colleagues) to the business community. Because these programs can be led by staff, they can be offered more easily than collaborative programs. You are your own best resource when it comes to programming. You know your patrons and you have skills that can get your programming off the ground.

But you can't do everything. And most of us, even those with business experience, are not qualified to teach all of the classes entrepreneurs need. Fear not, help is out there. Call on the people you know.

Budget concerns can affect how you program in all departments of your library. Keep in mind that while your library may pay for much of the programming offered to the general public, it is not always necessary to pay for your business programming. In fact, you can often host programs that cost little or no money.

Partners are an excellent source of speakers, panelists, and program leaders. Many local government and not-for-profit organizations will provide programming for little or no cost. These business organizations generally have a menu of programs they run throughout the year. Often these organizations are willing to provide the program off-site at your business center. These partners usually can market programs to people outside of your network. Partnering with these organizations for programming can help bring additional business patrons to the program and to your library.

The local entrepreneurs and businesspeople you work with are good sources for free or low-cost programming. While it can be a little trickier to set up with for-profit businesses, as many would like to promote their businesses, it can be highly beneficial to both parties. Programs led by bankers, insurance professionals, and social media experts or web designers can be educational and informative and not sell anything to the attendees. Since most libraries will not host programs that are sales pitches for outside products or services, be sure to remind the speaker that the program is topical and require that the speaker's product or service not be discussed. Check your library's policy and talk to your director about allowing speakers to hand out business cards or brochures at the end of the program to attendees who request them. This can have many benefits for your business center by allowing you to offer relevant programming and by strengthening your relationship with the businesses in your network.

Publishers and database providers are also a source for programming. Most publishers have assigned your library a local or inside sales rep. Utilizing these sales reps for programming can benefit in many ways. As a business librarian who uses the databases regularly, you are probably more than capable of leading an introductory program for any of them. Yet we know that often time is what we have the least amount of; so why not use all the resources at your fingertips?

Databases are an integral part of all library collections and offer a magnitude of information that will help entrepreneurs with funding, marketing, competitive intelligence, and more. Still, a database's worth is measured by its use. We have spent hours researching, reviewing, and using the resources we have added to our business library; but if the patrons do not use these resources, they are worthless. For the uninitiated, navigating a business database can be a herculean task. Contact your sales rep, and encourage them to visit your library in person or via webinar for training.

You may be thinking, this is all great advice but I need some concrete examples! Well we have them for you.

Program Ideas

Remember what we said earlier in the chapter about coming up with program topics? What kinds of business reference questions are you getting? Think about your business reference interviews. What books are most popular? What business books are having the highest circulation? When you attend local business meetings, what are people talking about?

Most of the librarians we have spoken to over the past decade agree on the most asked business reference question (or some variation of the same idea)—"I want to start a business. What do I do?" This one question can lead to many different business programming ideas.

Reference Question/Request: How do I start a business? How do I write a business plan? What should I do first?

These are some of the most basic programs you can offer and can cover almost any aspect of writing a business plan, licensing, corporate structure, and more. Any local Small Business Administration (SBA), Small Business Development Center (SBDC), or SCORE office can provide an instructor for programs like these. Business librarians can also lead a basic business plans program by focusing on the useful library resources for completing a plan.

How to Start a Small Business in Hoover

Starting a business can vary from location to location. Different towns and cities have different policies and procedures for getting a business off the ground. The Hoover Library in Hoover, Alabama, partnered with the town's Revenue Department to offer How to Start a Small Business in Hoover, and the patrons love it. Attendees are getting not only basic information on starting a business but also specifics on doing business in Hoover.

Entrepreneur Series

Since 2011, the New Haven Free Public Library (NHFPL) has offered a five-week Entrepreneurs Series a couple of times a year. Programs are held once a week and aim to help entrepreneurs create a business plan, understand basic financial statements, market their business traditionally and online, and work with the federal and state governments. NHFPL secured experts in each of these topics by partnering with local SCORE and SBA offices. Held in the evening from 5:30–8 p.m., each of the programs attracts 15–30 attendees.

Do You Have What It Takes to Be an Entrepreneur?

Many people want to quit the rat race and be their own boss, but most do not understand what being an entrepreneur entails. Starting your own business is a lot of work. While some may think the business will run itself and they can be semiretired, most know it may be a 24/7 endeavor. We've had people visit the Miller Center to find out about starting a business who are shocked at the amount of work it is to get off the ground. A program like this is a perfect introduction to the process. Led by a business counselor from our local SBDC, this program lays it all out for prospective entrepreneurs. The counselor does not hold back covering the steps and considerations in starting a business. In fact, sometimes it seems as if he is discouraging people from becoming entrepreneurs. Savvy attendees realize what he is doing and are not deterred. Those who are easily dissuaded save themselves (and their local business librarians) a lot of time and energy.

Reference Question/Request: I don't even know where to start when I look at your resources. Which database should I use to find my competitors?

Some types of preliminary industry, demographic, and competitive information needed by entrepreneurs can be easily found by them if they know how to use the resources you offer. Most of the librarians we spoke to during the course of writing this book offer programming that offers tutorials of their business resources.

Business Research Essentials

"Discover resources available that can help you make informed decisions about your business' future." The Portage District Library offers Business Research Essentials that show patrons how to use the library's collection to determine target market and locate competition and more information to help grow local business.

Introduction to BIZLINK

Offered several times throughout the year in the library and on location at various businesses, this program reviews the most popular databases available through BIZLINK, the Miller Business Center's collection of paid business databases.

EDUCATION
workshop

women's
EXPO

A marketplace of products
by **women entrepreneurs**

The Art of Promoting Yourself:
Perfecting Your Pitch

Thursday, September 10th
6:00pm - 8:00pm

Light Refreshments & Networking begin at 5:30pm

*Being able to describe yourself and your business is an integral part of
your personal brand tool-kit. Your "pitch" needs to convey a compelling
and memorable message that encourages your listener to take action
and make the discussion last longer.*

This workshop will help you:
Develop and deliver a "pitch" with confidence and credibility
Speak articulately and use appropriate body language
Communicate a clear and concise message

Register online today at
www.WomensEXPOli.org/workshop.html

FREE for Current/Previous EXPO exhibitors
Registration Fee - $15

Education Sponsor

This workshop takes place @
Middle Country Public Library - Centereach
101 Eastwood Blvd., Centereach, NY 11720
For more information, call 631-585-9393 x 296

Allstate.
Foundation

Figure 7.2 A typical Miller Center program flyer.

Competitive Intelligence

A great term to catch their eyes! Everyone wants to know what their
competitors are up to, but the term "competitive intelligence" sounds so
daunting to most. Using subscription databases and free resources, this
program shows how to gather information about competitors, including
company, executive, and industry information. Many attendees are

surprised at how much information they can find using subscription and targeted websites.

Reference Question/Request: Everyone says I should be on social media, but there are so many! Should I be on all of them? How can I keep up?

Introduction to Social Media for Business

This basic program can be easily taught by a business librarian. Start the program by going over best practices for social media for business. Review the business platforms (if available) for major social media platforms, including Facebook, Twitter, Instagram, and Snapchat, and discuss the strengths of each. For instance, Instagram is all about visuals. You can end the program with a discussion about which platforms would work best for the businesses in attendance.

Introduction to Facebook (or Instagram or Twitter—or Well You Get It)

Once you have offered a general program, consider offering individual programs for the platforms that were most popular. For instance, the Miller Center offers introductory classes in Facebook, Instagram, and Twitter. Each program reviews how to use the platform, related terms, and best practices.

Managing Social Media

After taking the introductory classes, we were still hearing from attendees that they felt overwhelmed by the need to post to social media regularly. How could they remember? What would they post? We began offering a program to help manage social media. The program discussed frequency of posts and ways to fill the posts, including using statistics, quotes, and news articles. We also introduced them to ways they could schedule posts using Hootsuite (our favorite at this moment).

Walk-In Wednesdays

So we've offered a general class on social media, introductory classes focusing on the major platforms, and a class on how to manage it all. We're done right? *Not so fast.* The feedback we were getting was that, while people were excited about social media immediately following a program, they often left the library and never set up an account. The task was just too daunting for many of them. We started Walk-In Wednesdays as a way to help with social media in a casual way. We certainly didn't want to become their social media managers but recognized that they needed a boost to get started. The program is very casual—the Miller Center business librarians hang out in the center with laptops and other mobile devices and business patrons drop in for help. We will walk them through setting up an account, posting, and scheduling. Sitting in a casual group allows for a lot of conversation among the librarians and entrepreneurs. Since its inception, this program has become much more broad covering questions about mail merge from MS Excel to how to use a specific database.

Once you've covered the basics, your patrons may be interested in going further with intermediate or advanced classes. Unless you are very proficient, you'll want to hire someone for these classes. Remember, when looking for instructors, think of the businesses you work with on a daily basis. Is there anyone you know who would be qualified?

Reference Question/Request: I have a hard time knowing how to introduce myself at networking events. How can I describe my business? How can I get my point across is a short time? (This is a great topic to cover as all businesspeople can benefit from successful networking.)

Perfecting Your Pitch: The Art of Selling Yourself

This program was created at the Miller Business Center in response to what librarians were seeing at various programs and events (See Figure 7.2). Many new entrepreneurs, when asked, were unable to articulate what their business was. Even for something as simple as a gluten-free bakery, the entrepreneurs were having a hard time encapsulating their business in a few sentences. Led by a professional trainer with stage experience, attendees were guided to ways to communicate a clear and concise message with confidence and credibility. The supportive environment and guidance resulted in significant changes in the ways entrepreneurs were introducing and presenting themselves in networking situations.

Reference Question/Request: Everyone tells me I should be on Etsy/ eBay/Amazon Handmade, but I don't even know how to get started.

Introduction to Etsy

We find that most entrepreneurs asking for this assistance truly are at the most beginning phases of starting and haven't even started investigating the services of these websites. A very basic Etsy class, covering creating an account, listing items, and promoting the page, can be taught by most librarians. To capitalize on the success of the program, offer one-on-one appointments to help attendees set up their accounts.

Figure 7.3 Success with an Etsy business banner ad.

Success with an Etsy Business

Held at the Mesa THINKspot at Red Mountain Library, Success with an Etsy Business focused on the experiences of successful Etsy sellers (See Figure 7.3). Attendees heard their stories, tips, and tricks and had the opportunity to share things they have learned. A program like this one is a great opportunity for entrepreneurs to meet others who are starting up an Etsy business. Librarians who do not personally know an Etsy seller can use Etsy's local search. Within each search is the ability to narrow down by location, which enabled THINKspot to put together their panel of local Etsy sellers.

Reference Question/Request: I keep hearing that <insert new technology here> can help my business, but I don't know much about it. Can you tell me?

New technologies whether it be software or hardware are being developed so quickly that it's often hard to keep up.

30 Apps in 60 Minutes

While this is not an original idea—you can find a program like this at many trade shows—it is one that is ideal for the business community. The apps chosen reflect the audience and focus on productivity, organization, travel, scheduling, and planning. Of course, some fun stuff is added at the end.

Because of the format, this program requires minimal preparation. A month or so before, solicit suggestions from friends, coworkers, and patrons. Some apps to consider are Google Drive, Tunity, Seat Guru, Canva, Slack, and Join.me. Most apps you feature should be free (or have a free component). Since you are only spending two minutes on each app, you do not need to be an expert on any of them. We offer this program at the Miller Center every year and have lots of fun with it. Attendees keep count and make sure we keep to our 60-minute limit. By the end, it becomes something of a race.

Design, Develop, DIY: 3-D Printing in the Twenty-First Century

Responding to questions from their business community, the Mount Prospect Public Library offered an informational program on 3-D printing. Taught by instructors from the local community college, the program showed the applications of 3-D printing and its software in the world today. They also covered different types of 3-D printers, how to create 3-D models, and samples of different projects. What new technologies you are reading about in professional journals, newspapers, and online? If you are reading or hearing about them, chances are your business patrons are as well. Find a way to share this information with your business community. Your library doesn't have to own a 3-D printer (although many of you probably do) or any of these other new technologies. Like the Mount Prospect Public Library, offer these programs as informational only. Think of which organizations might have the technologies and be willing to share their knowledge. A local college is a great place to start.

Reference Question/Request: Do you have the book that is number one on the *Wall Street Journal*'s business best-seller list? Can you recommend a title that might motivate me?

Business Book Clubs/Discussion Groups

As librarians, we have familiar book clubs and discussion groups. In fact, your library probably has a few, covering different topics; so why not a business book group? Choose popular business books and be sure to promote them using the standard information as well as its subject and themes. A businessperson might not see the appeal in reading *Who Moved My Cheese?* but could be interested in learning how to cope with change in the workplace. A recent program at the Miller Center discussing this title turned into a wonderful group discussion on people's experiences and strategies they utilized during times of heavy change.

Reference Question/Request: But really, what do you guys do here?

Open House

Yep, there will always be people who don't quite understand your service or the power it wields. A couple of years ago, the Miller Center began hosting an annual Open House. This casual event is a way to get people into the center and to introduce them to our staff and to each other. This low-key, two-hour program is one of the easiest we do at the center. There is no formal presentation. Business librarians mingle with attendees. This enables us to practice our elevator speeches and set up one-on-one appointments for full overviews.

While this was the first reason we started hosting an Open House, we have found that it has also become a way for us to thank our supporters. Many attend just to say "hi" while enjoying light refreshments. Ultimately it becomes a very easy way for us to provide another opportunity for business patrons to network with each other.

Reference Question/Request: I've signed up to exhibit at a local business trade show, but I've never even attended a trade show. Any tips?

Most businesspeople will attend or exhibit at a trade show sometime during their careers. Maybe even an event you host at your library! Whether a businessperson exhibitor just attends or not, there are many ways to maximize their time to yield the best results at the show. Consider a program covering the essentials of trade shows.

Strategies for Generating Traffic and Leads at Trade Shows

A marketing expert or seasoned trade show exhibitor can lead a program covering the basics of attending. This program gives strategies on what to do before, during, and after the show to maximize positive results. While offering a program like this, try to coincide it with a local business trade show.

Trade show programs can be especially helpful if you decide to host a trade show in your library. Offering these programs can increase interest in and success of your library's trade shows.

At this point you may be thinking, "Trade shows? At the library?" Trade shows do not have to be the elaborate, multiday events. We are calling them trade shows here, but perhaps if we call them expos or fairs, you will feel more comfortable. Better? OK, now do you think you might be able host one of those? You can! Your library can host a trade show for a few hours with some tables and table covers. Work with what you have. While it is great if you have a large meeting room that can accommodate it, but you can also consider hosting a fair on the public floor. Exhibit space can wrap around your existing shelving. One benefit to this arrangement is increased traffic. Not only will you get the people specifically looking for the event but also those using the library for other reasons.

Business Resource Open House

The Business Resource Open House, described by Jay Lyman as a "mini-fair," is held at the Seattle Public Library (SPL) and offers businesses and entrepreneurs the opportunity to meet experts in different fields. These experts include SCORE, SBA, and the local Office of Economic Development. Entrepreneurs and businesses that are looking for help with a business idea or financial concerns and more are invited to meet one-on-one with representatives from these organizations.

Keeping this "mini-fair" truly mini and limiting the number of organizations invited to participate enable Jay to offer it several times a year with more than 200 participating in 2016.

Entrepreneur Fair

In July 2015, Cherry Hill Public Library held its first Entrepreneur Fair. Working with a grant Cherry Hill received from LibraryLinkNJ, the New Jersey Library Cooperative and Technology and Entrepreneurship Talent Network of New Jersey, Andy Woodworth worked with local business organizations to offer entrepreneurs and business owners a one-stop opportunity to connect with resources and services that could take their businesses to the next level. Andy recruited 14 organizations and other resources, including the chamber of commerce, SCORE, and SBA to help more than 60 attendees who attended the Entrepreneur Fair. The response was great. Attendees ranged from people considering a foray into entrepreneurship to start-ups to established businesses.

Strictly Business

Now in its 10th year, the idea for the Miller Business Center's Strictly Business event started during a conversation with the local Brookhaven Coalition of Chambers. Knowing they wanted to work together on some project for Long Island businesses, the two organizations considered what was not being offered to their clients. While there were local trade shows, most were extremely small and hyper-local, which didn't give businesses much of an opportunity to network outside of their existing contacts. The area hosts one large business-to-business event. Held by a local business organization at the community college, this event boasts more than 250 exhibitors and over 2,000 attendees. However, booth space at this show was hundreds of dollars and cost prohibitive to most small businesses. In addition, the attendees were not the best market for smaller, local businesses.

A decision was made to hold a business-to-business trade show for the Brookhaven business community. Its goal would be to give small, local business the opportunity to network with each other and do some business. During the planning of the first event, the local chamber of commerce was brought into partnership and an additional goal was added—increase chamber membership. The organizations involved in the event believe in the power of networking and the strength of local chambers. Significant discounts on exhibit space, which was already relatively inexpensive, were offered to those businesses who were members of their chamber of commerce. This savings encouraged people to join their local chambers.

Figure 7.4 Strictly Business flyer.

When offering an event this large, we utilize the entire library—our patrons are very patient with us when it comes to events. Some of our shelving is wheeled off the public floor, and the space is filled with exhibit tables. In other spaces, exhibit tables hug shelving and wind around different spaces. It is a challenge to set it up so it flows, but after a lot of trial and error, we have a good system.

This event is a huge success for us, but it certainly didn't happen overnight. Or even in two years. We keep evaluating how we are doing and make changes. Each year, we refreshed the show to keep attendance up and continue to make it valuable for exhibitors (See Figure 7.4). In an effort to get attendees to visit both ends of the trade show floor, we have even created destination areas: on one end, the Café Corner featuring local food companies, and on the other, the Innovation Pavilion featuring cutting-edge companies and technology.

While the first Strictly Business featured just 30 exhibitors and 250 attendees, after 10 years, it now has topped out at 105 exhibitors (there's just not enough space in the library for more) (See Figure 7.5). The number of attendees grows each year and should reach 1,000 in its 10th year. All proceeds from the event support the Miller Business Center, the Brookhaven Coalition of Chambers, and the Greater Middle Country Chamber of Commerce. The most important result of this event is the new businesses we have introduced to the resources and programming of our business center.

Maybe a trade show isn't for your library. Perhaps you don't have the space, or there's another show that fills the bill for your area. That's OK. You should always be thinking of programming in terms of what would be most valuable to your community.

Still you should consider a big event of some kind that would appeal to your business community. Big events bring bigger attention to the library and its services. Keep in mind that big is relative to the size of your library and its business community.

The SPL knows how to host a big event. Three years ago, they were approached by a group who wanted to host a Startup Weekend (*https:/ startupweekend.org/*) at the library. Held throughout the country, Startup Weekends are three-day events that simulate the highs and lows of a real start-up. Groups of entrepreneurs or wannabes gather together to brainstorm, plan, and pitch a brand new company.

In that first year, the Startup Weekend was merely hosted at SPL. After experiencing the weekend and seeing how well it would fit with the other business services, Jay Lyman turned it into a library program.

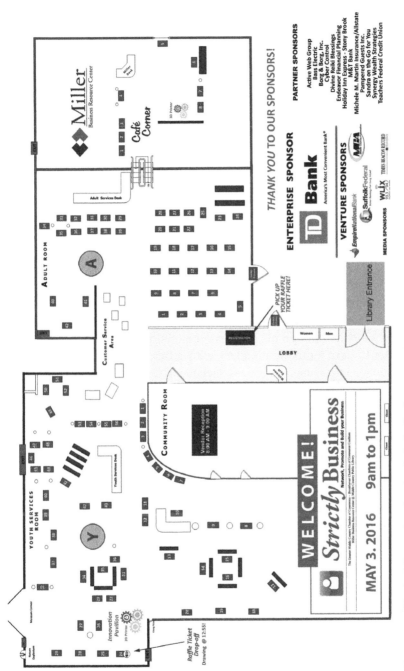

Figure 7.5 Typical floor plan for the Strictly Business event.

Startup Weekend EDU at SPL held its third annual event in 2016. The EDU indicates that their weekend focuses on new education products. Just fewer than 100 people participated in the weekend, which starts on a Friday night with strangers meeting and brainstorming with each other to come up with between 30–40 pitches for the group. Participants include educators, developers, designers, and entrepreneurs. After hearing the pitches, participants vote for the top 15 and form teams to turn pitches into plans. On Saturday, experts from the education and entrepreneurial worlds come in to help teams get their ideas off the ground. Teams go into the library to research markets and industries and are helped along the way by Jay and his team.

This is truly a full weekend event that takes over the library, with teams working until 10 p.m. or later on Saturday. Sunday morning is spent working with pitch coaches and other experts to refine presentations and perfect pitches. A panel of expert judges, including venture capitalists, edtech entrepreneurs, educators, and former Startup Weekend winners, is put together to choose the winning teams who receive prizes such as time with experts, pitch time with a venture capital firm, and coworking space.

Sounds daunting? Jay works with the Startup Weekend team to get funding and prize and find experts to assist teams and judge pitches. Beyond that he markets through his business connections and other organizations in order to have a mix of attendees with different backgrounds and skills. And, as we know, success breeds success. The more Startup Weekend EDU continues to grow and succeed, the higher the demand will be.

When planning a big event such as Strictly Business or Startup EDU, it is important to be organized. Although the stereotypical librarian is hyper-organized, we know in real life that is not always true. If you are not one of these librarians, you might want to invest in a project management class. While it is not necessary, it will help. At the Miller Center, we rely heavily on timelines to keep ourselves on track with all the events we are planning throughout the year. A simple timeline using Microsoft Word or Excel can help you and your team get everything covered for the big event (See Figure 7.6).

Keep thinking outside the box when it comes to programming. What do your patrons need? It is more than just offering the topics they want. Are your business patrons having a hard time getting into the library for programs? Maybe it's time to offer webinars that can be accessed from anywhere. Webinars can usually be saved for later viewing. Having archived webinars becomes a valuable tool when helping people who may have missed a program but still need the information. Rather than reviewing the basics of a program someone missed, having a recorded webinar gives you the opportunity to help the patron and save yourself some time.

STRICTLY BUSINESS PLANNING TIMELINE - STAFF		
	Task	**Staff**
	Contact major sponsors	SSM/EM
	Identify potential new sponsors	SSM/EM
	Confirm Strictly Business date	EM
	Book rooms/spaces in PRMS	DF
Jan-Feb	Revise Sponsor Packets	SSM/EM
	Revise Save-the-Date Flyer	SD
	Send Sponsor Packets to potential sponsors	SSM/EM
	Update website	SD
	Confirm Media Sponsors	SSM/EM
	Update Sponsors on website	SD
	Continue to contact sponsors	SSM/EM
	Attend local Chamber meetings to promote show	AB
	Contact all media partners to determine interest, types of promotion, and deadlines	SSM
March	Vendor mailing via Campaign Monitor	SD/AB
early March	Flyers to Suffolk Libraries	AB
	Begin posting on Media Sites	
	Café Corner mailing	MG
	Plan Trade Show workshop	EM
	Planning Committee Meeting	EM
	Confirm Sponsors and Planning Committee for Directory	EM
	Update website	SD
	Inventory supplies (tablecloths, balloons, tickets, etc.)	SD/AB
April	Table Inventory	SD/AB
	Continue posting on Media sites	
	Host Trade Show Workshop	SD/AB
	Update Media list	AB
	Constant Contact e-mail Strictly Business reminder EVERY WEEK	

Figure 7.6 Basic timeline for Strictly Business event.

	Update website	SD
	Planning Committee Meeting	
	Revise Floor Plan/Assign Vendor spaces	SD/AB/EM
	Print Posters (2- C & 1 - S)	
	Flyer distribution to all desks/buildings	EM
	Complete Directory	ALL
	Inventory and prepare event signage	EM/JR
	Sponsor Board (1)	
	Many Thanks Board (1) Planning Committee and other products	
	Parking directional signs	
	Handicapped parking signs	
	Strictly Biz signs for Eastwood and Middle Country Road	
	Request Banners from sponsors	EM
	Name tags for volunteers (designate Planning Committee as needed)	
	Vendor table signs	SD/AB
	Complete map (in-house)	EM/SD/AB
	Submit custodial workorders and map with table designations to John Miccoli	EM/SD/AB
	Submit computer services project forms	SD/AB
	Order tables from Mid-Island Rental (copy of PO to JM)	EM
	Contact sponsors re: photo @ 12 p.m.	SSM/EM
One week prior	Vendor e-mail with arrival instructions	SD/AB

Figure 7.6 (Continued)

Arlington Heights Memorial Library (AHML) offers Lunch Bytes webinars during lunch hour. Topics range from marketing to using the library's digital studio. According to business specialist Julie Kittredge, although relatively new, these webinars are very popular and continue to grow. AHML uses WebEx to deliver these webinars to their patrons, but there are a lot of options out there.

The examples listed above are a very small sampling of what can be done regarding programming for your business patrons. The possibilities are endless and must reflect your particular patron needs. It is great to read about other library's programs and try to recreate them in your library.

Believe us: we've gotten some great ideas talking with people for this book. Remember to rework it to fit what works for you. Successful programming involves a lot of trial and error and is changing all the time.

Everyone's time is important, but for a businessperson, time literally is money. Be sure that all flyers and press releases describe the program and how it would benefit the business community. If the program speaker is well known in the community, include his or her name and affiliation on the flyer.

If you've read this chapter and still do not see how you could possibly offer programs to your business patrons because of time, space, or funding, consider working with a local business organization that has programs for its members. You can still do a lot at this level—offer to help brainstorm ideas based on the work you do with business patrons, or offer to attend the programs and help with registration and other logistics. Request five minutes at the beginning of the program to talk about what you do for business at your library.

Your programs might not be successful from the start. It may take a lot of experimenting with topics, times, and speakers to get the right mix for your patrons. Keep trying different things and, most importantly, keep talking to your business patrons. You may never have a 100 percent success rate, but you will have business patrons who are happy with your efforts.

Remember This

Business programming is like your general programming—it should reflect the needs and wants of the population you are serving.

CHAPTER 8

Reaching Out Is (Not) Hard to Do

What you've created in your eyes is a world-class business collection and top-notch services for small business owners. Now what? It's time to get marketing. These are things that, as librarians, we may not think about regularly. That will have to change. If you are going to market your business reference services to small business owners, you have to think like a small business owner.

Hit the Pavement

We've mentioned it over and over throughout this book, yet it bears repeating—in order to have successful business services, you must go into the community to let them know who you are and what you do. If that means spending some time out of the library (and perhaps out of your comfort zone), so be it! The best way to meet potential patrons is attending local business meetings such as your local chamber of commerce, Rotary Club, or business networking group. You may have the challenge of convincing your director to let you out into the world, but believe us when we say that this will be one of the most important thing you will do as a business librarian: networking. In many cases, these meetings will take place either before or after the workday, giving you a bit of flexibility with your day's schedule. It's important to understand that the small business owners who are attending these meetings are also out of their office as well, away from running their business. You should expect these meetings to be brisk, and in many cases, informal.

Networking can be a very scary thought for many people. We get it. Meeting new people is hard. And we've all met some "professional" networkers who barely look at you before trying to sell you something. *Selling is not networking.* Networking is building and developing relationships that can become mutually beneficial in a business sense. Building relationships takes times, so while networking will result in new patrons, partnerships, and support, it is unlikely to happen right away. Be open and honest. Listen to the people you meet, and take an interest in what they do. Finding out more about the people you meet will spark ideas on how you can help them or how you can work together.

Many of the meetings you will attend will offer you the opportunity to network with the membership as well as take part in what is known in our neck of the woods as a "Round Robin." Each attendee is given 60 seconds or less to stand up, introduce themselves, and tell the room where they are from and what they do. (In business speak, this is sometimes referred to as the "Elevator Speech," in which in a hypothetical situation one is tasked with selling himself or herself in the time it takes to ride the elevator from the lobby to the top floor with the decision maker of a company.) It is best to practice your speech and to be as concise as possible. Here is an example:

> Good morning, my name is Sal DiVincenzo and I'm a business librarian at the Miller Business Center at the Middle Country Public Library. We provide local business owners such as yourselves with business research services such as industry information, demographics, market trends, and most importantly, access to lists of potential customers based on your custom criteria. We also offer informative programming geared toward small business owners as well as a number of networking events throughout the year. Best of all, there is no charge to use our services or attend our programs. So please see me afterward, and I'll be happy to further discuss what I can do for you and your business. Thank you, and I look forward to helping you make your business as successful as it can be.

Simple, concise, positive, and to the point. It's a great message and probably the easiest sales pitch you'll ever have to make. (If time permits, we might add another "Did I mention that it's all free?" to our speech, as it emphasizes the point for the financially conscious business owner as well as adds a little humor to our speech and usually gets a chuckle out of our audience.)

Terry Zarsky is the business librarian at the Penrose Place branch of the Pikes Peak Library District in Colorado Springs, Colorado, and has been supporting local small business owners for 30 years. Being the senior business librarian on staff, she has gained the reputation of being the "go-to" person when it comes to business resources. She's always busy. In addition to doing research for patrons, Terry is outside her office 15–25 days per month doing outreach for Pikes Peak at various organizations such as the local chambers of commerce, Regional Business Alliance, economic development agencies, and somewhat unique to her demographic, military bases.

Serving veterans in her community is a big part of what she does, especially now that "lots of bases are closing and vets are coming to us for help in starting a small business." She says that at least 20 percent of her business patrons are veterans looking to do business research. It's become so prevalent that she does a multiweek "Boots to Business" program that focuses on maneuvering veterans out of the military mind-set and into the small business world.

When speaking with Terry, she will be adamant to mention the importance of networking and outreach. She first went after the obvious choices: chambers of commerce, business development agencies, and the like. Through those venues she has been able to connect with other organizations, partly due to her zeal for networking and partly from connecting with attendees from other organizations. Her primary form of marketing the services of her branch and Library 21c is getting out there on a regular basis (almost daily!). Terry is blessed to have the support of her administration, which she feels is essential when doing outreach, as she is seldom sitting at a desk in the library. Time is also important, and having time as much as possible is essential. Terry is the sole business librarian at her branch, and she works incredibly hard to offer the best for her patrons. "Coming from a military family, I know what's necessary to get the job done ... you can't do this in 40 hours per week," she said.

Business Cards

Now that you are *the most popular person in the room*, be prepared to be asked for your business card. It's an important part of networking, and you'll want to make sure you have one. This doesn't mean that you have to hit up your director for cards, either. There is plenty of free software out there allowing you to create your own custom card. We are lucky enough to have separate business cards: one general card for the library, and one for the business center (See Figure 8.1). It is preferable to give out the card that mentions what you do (business research) as the folks you are meeting will be collecting a number of cards, and coming across a public library business card two weeks later might not ring any bells for them. There's nothing wrong with writing "Call me for business research" on your general library business card, either. Remember: get their card, too!

The more events you attend, the more cards you will collect. Make notes on each card as a reminder of what the person does or needs. This will help when you get back to office and can't remember who is who. This will also help with your follow-up.

ALEX BLEND
LIBRARIAN

MIDDLE COUNTRY PUBLIC LIBRARY
101 EASTWOOD BOULEVARD
CENTEREACH NY 11720-2745
blendalex@mcpl.lib.ny.us

TEL 631 585 9393 x272
FAX 631 585 5035
www.mcpl.lib.ny.us

Alex Blend
Information Specialist

Middle Country Public Library
101 Eastwood Blvd,
Centereach, NY 11720
Phone: 631-585-9393 ext. 272
Fax: 631-585-3670
Email: blendalex@middlecountrypubliclibrary.org
www.millerbusinesscenter.org

Figure 8.1 Consider separate business cards differentiating your regular services and your business library services.

Yes, follow-up! Don't collect business card just to be polite. Business cards are invaluable to the marketing of your business services. If you collect cards and leave them in your pocket only to find them the next time you wear that jacket, you are missing opportunities. Use the cards you collect to follow up. It doesn't have to be elaborate. A simple e-mail or phone call saying how nice it was to meet is sufficient. If you discussed anything specific, mention it. This will differentiate you from the other people they met at the event and is a solid step toward a good relationship.

Brochures

One powerful tool with getting the word out is a nicely designed brochure. You certainly do not need it to be printed on glossy paper or card stock; the most important thing will be the content. A nice mix of artwork and text is the way to go. Please don't use clip art. Please. If you can get away with a month's subscription to an image site such as clipart.com or use royalty-free photos, that would be optimal. Leave the four or five paragraphs of what you do for the meet and greet: your brochure should point out what you do boldly and succinctly, and again, throwing in the word "Free (or low cost) Service" greatly helps. Small business owners like takeaways. They are busy, they are on the go, and they are "do you have some additional information you can send me?" types of folks. Sending them home with your business card and brochure or flyer is a great first step (See Figure 8.2).

There may be a number of situations where you may not have the opportunity to network with business owners at a meeting; sometimes the stars

Your Business Can Never Be Too Successful

Whether you're big or small, the key to effective management, sustained growth, and healthy profit margins is having the right resources at your fingertips. That's what the Miller Business Resource Center is all about. Our expert staff will help you find industry facts, consumer trends, and other valuable business intelligence, as well as connect you with prospects and colleagues through our popular networking events.

The Miller Center serves as a regional resource for businesses, independent entrepreneurs, not-for-profit organizations, and individuals. It offers access to extensive and specialized business resources as well as personalized business research and reference assistance. The goal of the Center is to support regional economic development by meeting the information needs of the business community, promoting a literate and job-ready workforce, and providing employment information and career exploration opportunities. The Center sponsors networking and training events and works in partnership with Long Island business support organizations to provide greater public access to the information and services they offer.

Miller
Business Resource Center
@ Middle Country Public Library
101 Eastwood Blvd.
Centereach, NY 11720
631-585-9393

Miller Center Team

Elizabeth Malafi
Coordinator
malafielizabeth@middlecountrypubliclibrary.org
Ext. 296

Sal DiVincenzo
divincenzo@middlecountrypubliclibrary.org
Ext. 216

Marlene Gonzalez
gonzalezmarlene@middlecountrypubliclibrary.org
Ext. 215

Alex Blend
blendalex@middlecountrypubliclibrary.org
Ext. 272

Gilda Ramos
ramosgilda@middlecountrypubliclibrary.org
Ext. 248

Hours

Mon. - Fri. 9:30am to 9:00pm
Sat. 9:30am to 5:00pm
Sun. 1:00pm - 5:00pm

www.millerbusinesscenter.org

Figure 8.2 An in-house-produced brochure for the Miller Center.

don't align, and frankly, sometimes the moments will not be right. Having brochures and flyers to leave on a table or chair may be the best you can do that day, so it's so important to bring some with you.

As your business center grows and your services become more popular, you may have the opportunity to get the funding to have brochures professionally printed. Take our advice: if you do have that opportunity, take the time to plan what your brochure will look like and what should be included. The more general your design and content, the longer your brochure will last. For example, try not to use images that may look dated in a year. It's amazing how quickly that haircut goes out of style.

Be creative with something as simple as size. If you have permission from your director to spend the money on a professional brochure, why not do something outside the box? We've all been handed a trifold brochure printed on 8 ½ × 11 paper—double sided, semigloss finish—with an image on the front and the company name and the address on the back lower third. Yawn. Perhaps something square, something that opens up like a flower to reveal your services floating on a sea of crisp dollar bills, with the word "free" embossed in block letters. You get the idea.

Attending Business Trade Shows

What better way to connect with as many local businesses as possible than to go where they are all gathered for hours at a time and all under one roof? There's something both exhilarating and intimidating about attending a business trade show. If you haven't had this opportunity, we highly recommend the experience. Many of the shows that we have visited are free to attend, especially if you preregister. This will be your opportunity to engage with potentially hundreds of businesses of various sizes. There will be a ton of giveaways at these things, so grab the bag they usually hand out at the entrance and fill it up with the business cards you collect, company brochures, and those little promotional materials: besides getting another potato chip bag clip for home, your eight key chain flashlights, and your 331st pen with a company name on it, this is a great place to gather ideas about your own marketing materials. While we already mentioned the concept of hosting your own trade show or business expo at your library, exhibiting at a business trade show is also a great idea. In many cases, there will be a cost involved with exhibiting, but do your due diligence to see if there is an opportunity to get a discounted exhibition fee or even a free table. The fact that you are providing such a valuable, free or low-cost service to local business owners, and you are a not-for-profit, should allow you some flexibility. Think outside the box, as well: perhaps the organization that is hosting the trade show would be interested in you becoming a partner. While you probably do not have the funds to be an official partner or sponsor, you are an important part of the business community, supporting local businesses. It's really within the best interests of any organization running a business trade show to feature such a wonderful resource to the business community.

We won't lie to you here: exhibiting at a trade show can be *brutal*. There is a certain etiquette that's required at these things; one that specifically comes to mind is while at your booth, you should always be standing up. Now we don't know about you, but being librarians we are accustomed to the comfort of the reference desk and the wonderful, hopefully comfy, chairs that we sit in for the majority of our workdays. Standing for upward of six hours, smiling, chatting, saying hello to anyone who passes your booth, which in some cases could be hundreds or thousands of faces, and hearing the question, "What is it exactly that you do?" is probably not what any of us is used to.

There will be a lot of prep work involved as well. Whether or not you have the budget for a giveaway, you will have to have something to give attendees, even if it is as simple as a printed handout. Signage will be very important. We like to put a bowl of candy out on our table, because invariably someone will come to grab a piece and it's a great opportunity to start a conversation. Don't be dissuaded by candy snatchers and give-away grabbers. They will come to your table, load their bag, and disappear into the throng of people, without even looking at you—they always attend these things. Keep any really sweet giveaways like those mugs with the library logo on it under the table for special guests who spend time chatting with you about your services.

Believe us when we say that at the end of a trade show day, the shoes are flung across the room, collapsing on couches, and some form of libation is usually consumed. But let us tell you: it is totally worth it. Some of your busiest times will be right after a trade show.

The simple fact is a trade show or business expo will be one of your best opportunities to get the word out on who you are and what you do. Do more than one of them, and you'll start to recognize faces and start to make relationships with local business owners, maybe even make a friend or two. The more you get out there, the more comfortable you will become. You may even have some fun.

People to Know Plus Great Places to Look for Networking Opportunities

- **Local Chambers of Commerce**—Attending your local chamber of commerce is a no-brainer. This is usually where you will find most of your neighborhood's small business owners. From our personal experience, we've had great success in getting the word out at these meetings. Many chambers will start off with some sort of roll call in which each attendee will get up and have 30–45 seconds to introduce themselves. Come prepared with a great elevator speech, flyers, and business cards. There's also usually some sort of food, so you got that going for you.
- **Rotary Club**—Many local businesses will be involved in the Rotary. This community support organization is a great place for you to remind

the members that you are in the business of support. Check your local Rotary's schedule for meetings that are specifically for networking.

- **Civic Associations**—While not a business organization per se, you may find local business owners or individuals looking to start a business attend civic meetings. Additionally, if a new business is coming into town, they usually send someone to the civic association to butter up the community.

- **Business Networking Groups**—Simply do a Google search for your local business networking groups, and you'll have a great start. Do your due diligence while researching to make sure that whatever group you intend to visit is appropriate. Some business networking groups are very strict: "members only" or "must bring at least two potential contacts." BNI International, a worldwide networking and referral group for example, requires 100 percent attendance or you are not eligible. No kidding.

- **Local Small Business Development Agency**—If you are not involved with your local small business development agency (SBDA), you are doing your library a great disservice. Besides being a great source for networking opportunities, your local agency will be staffed with at least one business counselor: folks who are certified to help small business owners with information on writing their business plans, find financing, learn how to market themselves, and much more. Additionally, your local SBDA will most likely offer both you and your patrons with the opportunity to attend education seminars for free. We treat our local office, the Stony Brook Small Business Development Center, as partners and an integral part of what we do for our business community. If you haven't already reached out to them, put this book down and call them right now. We'll be here when you get back,

- **SCORE**—Once known as Service Corps of Retired Executives, SCORE is a nonprofit organization supported by the Small Business Administration (SBA). Retired business owners, CEOs, and managers act as mentors for budding entrepreneurs. Counseling is free, and many times SCORE will meet with their clients in the library. SCORE also provides free workshops that can either take place at their base of operations (many times a government building) or your library.

- **Local SBA Office**—The SBA is another organization that you should reach out to as soon as possible. Besides the wealth of services that they provide, they will also be a great means of traveling along other paths to referrals, finding networking opportunities, and connecting with other local agencies that we may not have mentioned here. They will also be one of the go-to agencies for patrons who are looking for funding: there is lots of money available to loan out there, and the organization will have easy-to-follow resources on how to apply for SBA loans.

- **Offices of Economic Development**—Reaching out to your local offices of economic development in your town or county is important. Again, from personal experience, our local office is considered a partner in what we do. Many times they will come to us for demographic data, either for themselves if they are doing any economic reporting to the local news agencies or for the government. Additionally, we will go to them to make contacts with other potential agencies and in many cases, local government officials. From time to time, your office may sponsor a job or business fair: be part of it.

- **Nonprofits**—Have any big nonprofit organizations in your community? Connect with the organization's event person. Many times local businesses will partner with local social services organizations. If you are involved, you can make a connection. Many times nonprofits are looking for partners for campaigns or events. It's a good way to get a free table so you can put your flyers/wares out for your community to see. Remember: local business owners and entrepreneurs have families and friends. Increasing your exposure in your neighborhood by any means necessary should be first priority, and if you can do it for free, it's a bonus.

Marketing your services never ends. Use these ideas either as a whole or in parts to find the sweet spot for you and your library. Don't be discouraged if you don't start off with hundreds of businesses knocking down your door. Persevere and word will spread. People will start to see the library as an important part of their business success.

Remember This

We'll say it again; get out of the library to meet the businesspeople.

CHAPTER 9

Stories from the Front Line

We've reviewed ideas for you to use to begin or expand your work with your local businesses. We've included many real-life examples from libraries throughout the country, but it still only scratches the surface of what you will encounter as you get deeper into the business community. This chapter includes some of our memorable business patron interactions. We hope they will show you how varied the reference work of business librarians can be. We also hope you will see how rewarding it is to help a businessperson add to your community's economic engine.

Certain details such as names, locations, and affiliations have been changed or omitted out of respect for privacy or to protect a patron's intellectual property.

Mr. Pizza

A gentleman came to the reference desk with a delicious request. He received prize money and was looking at opening up his own pizzeria. More specifically, he was looking at purchasing an existing pizzeria and had a choice between two very distinct neighborhoods. He wanted to get as much information as possible about those locations to better decide which would be the most profitable. During the reference interview, we came to find out that he was a finalist of a national pizza-making competition sponsored by one of the major cable networks. He was hoping to ride the wave of his success to starting his own business. There were a couple of approaches that we made to help him gather this information. In the end, we used two resources to answer his question.

For those of you who live outside of New York: pizza is a serious business here, and not unlike Starbucks, it seems like there is a pizzeria every mile on Long Island. So the first thing we wanted to do is see how other pizzerias were doing in terms of sales around those locations. Using ReferenceUSA, we used their "Map Based Search" feature to draw a 10-mile radius around each potential location. We then added a search criterion of pizzeria as well as Italian restaurant, to be fully inclusive of that style of dining. We then used that data to compare how like-type businesses were fairing in those locations. We were also able to see how those exact locations were doing as well, just in case our patron did not already know (which frankly, he should have asked his agent!).

Next, we used DemographicsNow to look for consumer expenditure data. Thankfully, this database had "Pizza" as one of the metrics. We selected the closest zip codes to each location and ran a "Comparison Report" to see which locations had consumers more likely to spend more on pizza. Additionally, we compiled a package of reports for each location and surrounding area focusing on household income, daytime population, and demographic summary, including average age and family size.

We presented this information to the patron a few days later, and he was happy to have this data to make an important decision easier. What we found is that there was a very distinct difference between the two neighborhoods as far as average income, but not so much in terms of how much folks spent annually on pizza. The patron ended up selecting the location that had a lower household income, since his thought was much of what he would offer in terms of food would have a lower price point and be more appealing to that demographic.

He returned a few months after securing his spot for another request. He wanted to send out a postcard announcing his grand opening and offering a coupon. Once again using ReferenceUSA, this time utilizing their consumer database, we were able to target households very close to his new location and created a list of addresses for him to use in a mail merge. This scenario is a good example of using multiple resources as well as thinking about the big picture, to come up with data that would be useful for a small business owner.

As successful as our search for helpful data was for this patron, unfortunately his business was not. We hadn't heard from him for about a year before he touched base with us to let us know that he was no longer running the pizzeria but had moved on to being the head pizza maker at another successful existing pizzeria. It's rough out there in the world of small business, especially when you are in the restaurant business.

What may seem like a brilliant idea from someone who was smart enough to come to us for these data, there's always the chance that in the end, things won't go so well. The point is we do our absolute best to help everyone who comes to us for assistance. In the end, this business failed, but we were happy to hear that this patron ended up being very successful and happy making pizzas at someone else's existing business.

Our Very Own Dunder Mifflin

Sometimes a super easy project ends up with the greatest rewards. Having heard about us from a business association, a medium-sized, family-owned office supply company whose primary product was paper and boxes called the center to find out how we can help expand their business. They had just hired a number of new sales people, and they were dividing up Long Island into regions and sending the salesforce out to drum up business. At this point, the company was doing well maintaining their current client base and working to expand from referrals. The son of the owner was given the task of "thinking outside their comfort zone" and expand the business to locations not yet served, and types of businesses not yet served.

When they came to us and told us what they do and what their product was, our first thought was "Who needs paper and boxes?" When you think about it, lots of businesses need boxes, and most businesses, if not all, need some sort of paper. But this was a new venture for them; they had been comfortable dealing with their existing client base, and quite frankly, according to them, it was enough to support them. Now they wanted to go outside their comfort zone and send their new salesforce out to places they've never been before. The approach to this task was "Let's not target everyone in these areas, but those who were most likely to purchase your products based on their size and revenue." Using Mergent Intellect we were able to look at specific zip codes and specific types of companies who made more than $1 million a year and were part of industries that required new boxes: wholesale manufacturers and distributors. As a side project we also targeted very niche industries: places where boxes might come in handy, such as libraries! About once a month, we'd hear from the company asking for a different set of zip codes. Most of the company's targeting was the East End of Long Island—think the Hamptons out to the tip of the island where it meets the Atlantic.

It's not often that a patron calls just to say "hi," but the phone call we received from the paper company is one that we are so happy to get. The owner's son called to thank us for all the hard work we did in compiling the data and the lists of potential customers. He wanted to let us know that based on the research we had done for them, his salespeople were able to create over $250,000 worth of new business!

For us, it was a straightforward search for business types in a specific area. For them, it was an eye-opening and valuable decision.

The Kids These Days with Their Music and Their Shampoo

A young inventor was referred to us by the local Small Business Development Center (SBDC) who was in the process of writing his business plan. He had created a line of hair care products targeted toward millennials. He was specifically interested in market share information for the country's top shampoos and conditioners. In addition to the most recent market share data, he also wanted to know historical data so he can measure trends over certain brands. Now there are many challenges with this request, not because those data are not available, but because it can be hidden in other databases. The key here was going a little further, perhaps digging a little deeper.

This is where the reference interview came into play; the first question we asked was "What the heck is a millennial shampoo anyway?" The patron graciously let us in on his ideas, which were fascinating. We wish we could share them here, but hopefully his products will end up in the marketplace and you can say you vaguely remember reading that somewhere. After his explanation, we were able to offer more to him to supplement his original request. This is what makes a good business librarian a great one. We started with Gale Business Insights, which contains deep within the invaluable Market Share Reports. Using several years of these reports, the patron was able to extrapolate the data he needed and create charts that illustrated his place in the market for his business plan.

We once again dug into the DemographicsNow resource to find nationwide and local consumer expenditures for hair care products, soaps, and body washes. We used First Research to get an industry profile of the hair care product industry, which includes a five-year projection of that industry's growth as well as great financial information and key concerns to executives and managers.

Now that we've discovered the Standard Industry Classification (SIC) code for that industry, we were able to take a look at similar type companies in our region to see if (1) they existed and (2) what kind of revenue they had. We also did a quick search in Business Source Premier for any articles about millennials, purchasing habits, and hair care products. We packaged it all up in PDFs and sent it over. The patron was overwhelmed by the response and the quantity of data we were able to find, and incredibly thankful as well.

One of the points that we want to make telling this story is that while you might not have every resource we listed here available to you, there are many avenues you can go down to find something that would be helpful. In many cases, your patron will be starting out with nothing, so even something as simple as articles about their industry can be incredibly helpful.

Give Us Four Days and We'll Give You the United States

Sometimes getting the answers for small business owners is just a matter of asking specific questions, organizing your time, and traveling down the great, big broadband highway. And other times it's not only easy but also very informative. A gentleman who owns an employee benefit business had an interesting request. He had found that there was potentially a way to get e-mail addresses for every single licensed insurance agent in New York State. He did this by making a FOIA request, or a Freedom of Information Act request, with the regulating agency in New York. He was unsure if we would have similar information on a national scale, since it is technically public record but not easily accessible. We unfortunately do not have a go-to database for a list of insurance salespeople and their e-mail addresses. This is where the reference interview is so incredibly important: after some back and forth, as well as some poking and prodding around the web, we were able to find that there was a path, albeit not as straightforward, to getting this information. We do our best to let our patrons know they should have realistic expectations when it comes to what's available out there, how quickly it can be obtained, and in this case, what kind of legal hurdles there might be getting this information. In this situation, the business owner did not want us to obtain the lists for him (thankfully). What he really wanted was information on each state's policies, procedure, and under which regulatory department this information was held.

Since we were dealing with the entire United States, we broke the country down in sections, first concentrating on the largest states and then focusing on regions. Each week for three weeks, we would visit each state's regulatory sites, FOIA information pages, and open records or public records pages and gather the information. We then inserted the data into a spreadsheet that included contact information along with links, if available, to forms for requesting the information. In some cases, it was unclear how someone would make such a request. In other cases, the states published the data right on their websites! In fact, both Georgia and Nevada had downloadable Excel spreadsheets that included name, address, and e-mail addresses of every insurance salesperson in their state as well as agents from other states who could practice in their state. The patron was thrilled, and so were we. It was an incredible learning experience: navigating through each state's Department of Insurance website, seeing how each state handles requests for open records, and quite frankly, seeing which states seemed to have their stuff together and others who did not.

This project did something else for us: it allowed us to learn that in many cases, information that we thought might not be readily available is available. Not only that, there are resources that are completely free and very valuable: the Georgia list of insurance agents and e-mails alone contained well over 100,000 records. For a small business owner, *that's the jackpot.*

From the Top Down

Not so much an individual story per se, but an important one to mention here nonetheless. We must once again emphasize the importance of sometimes thinking outside the box. When we first started getting requests about information regarding business centers, industrial parks, and dense commercial areas, there were no fancy mapping features available on the databases we subscribed to. We came up with an idea that used a number of different tools that, when used in concert, created usable data for our patrons.

It's a common request: "Is it possible to get a list of all the businesses in the Heartland Executive Park?" or "Can I get a listing of businesses along the Route 110 corridor?" At the time, the means in which we could gather these data was, for the lack of a better term, *clunky.* First we would take a look at a map, find street names, and then do a targeted search on that address.

In other cases, we would try radius searches from a fixed location; but when doing so, there are chances that you'd get other businesses outside your target area. You'd be surprised how many patrons do not understand the concept of "10-mile radius" or "20 miles from." We have a unique situation here on Long Island, in that if we were to do a 20-mile radius search from a zip code on the north shore of the island, we'd not only get all the businesses across the width of the island (good) but also businesses across the Long Island Sound on the Connecticut coast (bad). Up until a few years ago, we didn't have the ability to use the wonderful mapping features of databases such as ReferenceUSA and Mergent Intellect, which we will get to shortly.

Instead, we took a creative, and albeit lengthy, approach to this type of research. In the case of an industrial park or business center, we figured that it should be easy to pick out an area of concrete and buildings from, let's say, a satellite photo. So this got us thinking: what if we used satellite imagery to assist in finding businesses? With the advent of Google Maps,

Mapquest, Yahoo Maps, and the like, we can easily view satellite imagery and even better, overlay street names and towns on top of that view.

Take for example, the largest industrial park east of the Mississippi, the Hauppauge Industrial Park, which incidentally is on Long Island. When viewing a satellite image on Google Maps, it is incredibly easy to pick out.

Today, we can use the aforementioned mapping feature on ReferenceUSA to draw a polygon around the park and easy-peasy list of businesses inside the park. But back in the day we did it a little differently, and the reason why we bring this up is because you might not have access to some databases that have this feature, and perhaps you can use this method to get the data you need for your patrons.

At the time, we had to take a broader approach to our search, so since we'd have an idea of where the business center or industrial park was, we would start with a zip code search. Now granted at this point, we are getting all the businesses in that zip code, but stick with us; this is where the thinking-outside-the-box comes in. We would take the list of those businesses and import it into mapping software. In our case we used Microsoft MapPoint, but today there are a number of software packages available, and some of them are free to a point, such as BatchGeo (*www.batchgeo.com*), ZeeMaps (*www.zeemaps.com*), and ESRI (*www.esri.com*).

BatchGeo, for example, is an online mapping service that allows users to upload data in csv or xls format. The system magically extracts the necessary information and plots points on a map, which you can then export, share, or edit. While their "Pro" service carries at $99 per year cost, users can take the service for a spin and do 250 records at a time for free.

For this particular project, we would have needed more than 250 records anyway, so using MapPoint, we overlaid our results file onto a satellite map. Then, we "cut out" the industrial park using a polygon tool. Finally, all the results that fell inside that polygon were exported back out of the software and into our spreadsheet. The whole process took approximately two days, and there were times when our food and water ran out. Not really. But while it did take some time from start to finish, the results were positive. We had a list of all the businesses in the industrial park, a hotbed of activity and a common request from our patrons. Additionally, we made it a point to proactively run lists of all the industrial parks we knew of (or could pick out from space) and make lists for reference.

Today, mapping features are standard in the big business listing databases, and it's an incredibly easy task to find those big blocks of concrete, draw boxes around them and download lists. This also brings up another point:

thinking ahead. As you start to nurture relationships with the small business owners in your community, you will probably see a pattern in your requests for information. It might be a good idea to create premade packages of information. Do you have an industrial park in your community? Get a list of all the businesses inside the park. Your patrons will eat it up. And speaking of eating . . .

Cookies for Everyone

An elder woman came to the Miller Center in search of a source for bulk purchases of aluminum trays. She said she had been buying them at the local grocery store, but now that her cookies were selling, she needed to find a way to purchase them in bulk. Cookies, you say? Please tell us more.

Before even delving into what resources and organizations might help, we sat down to find out more about this woman and her business. It's a tale as old as time—woman bakes cookies. Friends and family love them. Say, "You should sell these. You would make a fortune." Woman says, "Why not?" She started in her kitchen making alfajores, a *dulce de leche* cookie she learned to bake in her home country of Peru. Sales were to her friends and friends of friends. Positive word of mouth resulted in exponential growth, and soon she was baking dozens of cookies each day.

After learning her story and tasting the alfajores, we came up with a game plan. Most importantly, she had to get out of her kitchen and become a legal business entity. By connecting with the local SBDC, we were able to get her on the right track as far as business set-up was concerned. They were also able to refer her to their Kitchen Incubator, which would allow her to use a commercial kitchen with all the proper licensing.

Using ThomasNet (http:/www.thomasnet.com/), a free online directory of more than 700,000 suppliers, we were able to find many local suppliers of packaging for her cookies. We also used ReferenceUSA to find local restaurant suppliers that she could visit.

After a few weeks, she returned (with more cookies) and said she was ready to really get out into the marketplace. We researched local farmers' markets on the U.S. Department of Agriculture's National Farmer's Market Directory (*https:/www.ams.usda.gov/local-food-directories/farmers-markets*) that may allow local foodstuffs. Other venues to sell include local craft or trade shows. As you will find, there is no one-stop source for these. Much of that information was gathered through simple Google searches and by speaking with other entrepreneurs. This is a great example of how having a network of entrepreneurs can help.

After finding venues for her to set up shop and sell her alfajores, we considered retail stores that might be good options for her. Using ReferenceUSA and Mergent Intellect, we found a list of local gourmet food stores and contact information for some bigger stores such as Whole Foods and Trader Joe's.

Over the next several months and years, we saw her business grow and grow. She consistently exhibited at local shows and farmers' markets, and after some packaging changes, she became a local vendor at our area's Whole Foods. Most importantly, every time she visited us at the center, she brought alfajores. *Delicioso!*

Postcards from the Edger

A start-up landscaper wanted to get the word out in his neighborhood that he was ready for business. Initially he wanted to send out a postcard to everyone within a 20-mile radius of his location (which incidentally was his home). First off, we felt it necessary to illustrate what a 20-mile radius looks like on a map, and in this case, we used ReferenceUSA's Consumer and Lifestyles module to do so. This module is a fantastic means of finding consumers in a specific geography based on their purchase behaviors. We also use it for general searches for households, and in this case, it would work well. After seeing the huge swath of yellow on the screen, the patron decided that 20 miles would be too much, and we adjusted the search area down accordingly. This brings up a point that we must reiterate: your guidance as a business librarian is incredibly important, and you must not be afraid to be firm with some of your patrons. In some cases, you may be asked for information with arbitrary criteria: *about a 20-mile* radius, *more than one* employee, or our favorite "*all* the companies in *this* county." You certainly do not want to waste your time, and frankly, you do not want your patron to waste his or her time either. We believe in quality over quantity, so when patrons have specific criteria for a search, we work with them to tweak and adjust their criteria so they are getting the most concise information possible.

In this case, we used a map-based search to build a box around the landscaper's neighborhood. Since he was targeting households, we excluded any retail/business areas, which are easy to see when using the "satellite" view. We also added additional criteria of homeowners who made more than $100,000 per year in annual household income, since we wanted to target homeowners who made enough money to afford his services (this was a mutually agreed upon number based on his zip code). Finally, we made sure to return only one contact per household, so his list would not include duplicates. After downloading his list, we did a quick format for a mail merge and sent him on his way. He had the names of approximately

250 potential customers, and his plan was to print address labels and send them an introductory coupon. We hadn't heard back from him since then; *hopefully he's been too busy cutting lawns.*

Remember This

Reference questions are as varied as the patrons you help. No matter how long you are in the business, you will always be asked new questions.

Conclusion: Did You Get All That?

Providing services to business patrons is a gradual process. Do not expect to read this book and put every idea, suggestion, and example in motion at your library. What we hope for the most is that we have helped you all feel more comfortable in your role as a business librarian and that you realize there are so many resources out there to help you along in your new and exciting business adventure.

Advocate

While more and more libraries are offering business services, it can still be a challenge to get the complete support of your administration and colleagues. You should always be advocating for the services you offer. One way to really show how valuable the services are is to collect success stories from the businesses you've helped. Share them with others in your library so they can continue to understand the value of what you are doing.

Get Involved

You've done a lot to get up-to-speed in business reference and services. You are attending conferences, talking with other business librarians in your area, and reading books like this one, but don't stop there. Get involved with a local or national group of business librarians. Share the knowledge you have acquired with a new batch of newbie business librarians.

Keep Learning

So you are finally comfortable with business reference and services. Your programming has good turnout, and you are meeting one-on-one with three or more businesses a week. You finally feel like you are running a successful business center. It is easy to say, "Whew, I'm done. I can relax now and just coast," but don't. Keep learning. Reread Chapter 1, The Business Librarian, and continue to hone your skills, expand your re-sources, and grow your network.

The Miller Business Center at the Middle Country Public Library has been working with businesses for more than a decade. While we started off in other careers, once we became business librarians, we worked hard to learn and understand the needs of our local entrepreneurial and business population. While we are light-years ahead of where we had been, we never stop learning and growing.

Bibliography

Aarons-Mele, Morra. "Why We Need to Tell Different Stories about Entrepreneurs." Accessed November 30, 2016. http://www.wsj.com/articles/why-we-need-to-tell-different-stories-about-entrepreneurs-1479697620.

Alvarez, Barbara. 2015. "Working Outside the Box: Meeting the Needs of Entrepreneurs." Accessed August 26, 2016. http://publiclibrariesonline.org/2015/03/working-outside-the-box-meeting-the-needs-of-entrepreneurs/.

American Library Association (ALA). 2015. "State of America's Libraries Report 2015." Accessed August 26, 2016. http://www.ala.org/news/state-americas-libraries-report-2015.

American Library Association (ALA). 2016. "The People's Incubator: Libraries Propel Entrepreneurship." Accessed August 26, 2016. http://www.ala.org/news/press-releases/2016/06/new-ala-report-highlights-libraries-engines-entrepreneurship.

Badger, Emily. 2013. "Why Libraries Should Be the Next Great Start-Up Incubators." Accessed August 26, 2016. http://www.citylab.com/work/2013/02/why-libraries-should-be-next-great-startup-incubators/4733/.

Basic Books. *The Best Business Books Ever: The Most Influential Management Books You'll Never Have Time to Read*. New York: Basic Books, 2011.

Business Reference and Services Section (BRASS). 2016. Business Reference and Services Section (BRASS) homepage. Accessed August 26, 2016. http://www.ala.org/rusa/sections/brass.

Cockerell, Lee. *The Customer Rules: The 39 Essential Rules for Delivering Sensational Service*. New York: Crown Business, 2013.

Collins, Bradley. 2012. "How Public Libraries Are a Boon to Small Business." Accessed June 19, 2016. https://americanlibrariesmagazine.org/2012/08/13/how-public-libraries-are-a-boon-to-small-business/.

Covert, Jack, and Todd Sattersten. *100 Best Business Books of All Time: What They Say, Why They Matter, and How They Can Help You*. New York: Portfolio, 2016.

Cruz, Rebecca. 2013. "Conducting Business in the Library." Accessed June 19, 2016. http://publiclibrariesonline.org/2013/03/conducting-business-in-the-library/.

Dalton, Meg. 2016. "Libraries Fill Vital Role in Changing Economy." Accessed August 26, 2016. http://www.greenwichtime.com/business/article/Libraries-fill-vital-role-in-changing-economy-7384338.php.

Dill. 2013. "A Non-Hipster Approach to a Co-Working Space." Accessed August 25, 2016. https://www.inc.com/kathryn-dill/beyond-the-books-arizona-libraries-welcome-new-entrepreneurs.html.

Forte, Eric, and Michael Oppenheim. *The Basic Business Library: Core Resources and Services*, 5th ed. Santa Barbara, CA: Libraries Unlimited, 2012.

Google. 2016. "Google Apps Learning Center." Accessed August 25, 2016. https://apps.google.com/learning-center/products/drive/#/list.

Google. 2016. "Google Analytics." Accessed August 26, 2016. https://analytics.google.com.

Haber, Steve. 2011. "Changing Role of Libraries in a Digital Age." Accessed August 26, 2016. http://www.huffingtonpost.com/steve-haber/the-changing-role-of-libr_b_803722.html.

Hamilton, Anita. 2014. "The Public Library Wants to Be Your Office." Accessed
    August 26, 2016. http://www.fastcompany.com/3034143/the-public-library
    -wants-to-be-your-office.

Hankins, Gary. *The Power of the Pitch*. New York: Kaplan Publishing, 2005.

Hoover Library. 2016. "Hoover Library Business Memberships." Accessed
    August 26, 2016. http://www.hooverlibrary.org/memberships#business.

Investopedia. 2017. "Elevator Pitch Definition." Accessed January 30, 2017.
    http://www.investopedia.com/terms/e/elevatorpitch.asp#ixzz4XHA4iDjr.

James, Geoffrey. 2015. "7 Short Books Worth More Than an MBA." Accessed
    November 1, 2016. http://www.inc.com/geoffrey-james/7-short-books
    -worth-more-than-an-mba.html.

McKay, Peter. 2017. "Business Books: Core Collections." Accessed February 10,
    2017. http://businesslibrary.uflib.ufl.edu/businessbooks.

McKendrick, Joe. 2013. "New Role for Public Libraries: Small Business Incu-
    bators." Accessed August 26, 2016. http://www.zdnet.com/article/new-role
    -for-public-libraries-small-business-incubators/.

Miami-Dade Public Library System. 2014. "Coworking at the Library." Accessed
    August 26, 2016. https://www.newschallenge.org/challenge/libraries/
    winners/101-coworking-at-the-public-library.

Microsoft. 2015. "Microsoft Knowledge Base." Accessed August 26, 2016.
    https://support.microsoft.com/en-us.

Moss, Rita, and David G. Ernsthausen. *Strauss's Handbook of Business Infor-
    mation: A Guide for Librarians, Students and Researchers*, 3rd ed. Santa
    Barbara, CA: Libraries Unlimited, 2012.

Pickett, Carmelita, and Steven Smith. 2011. "Avoiding the Path to Obsolescence."
    Accessed August 26, 2016. https://americanlibrariesmagazine.org/2011/09/
    05/avoiding-the-path-to-obsolescence/.

Prato, Stephanie. 2013. "What Is Entrepreneurial Librarianship?" Accessed
    August 26, 2016. http://infospace.ischool.syr.edu/2013/06/05/what-is
    -entrepreneurial-librarianship/.

Rainie, Lee. 2012. "Libraries Transformed: Research on the Changing Role of
    Libraries." Accessed August 26, 2016. http://www.pewinternet.org/2012/10/
    23/libraries-transformed-research-on-the-changing-role-of-libraries/.

Rainie, Lee. 2016. "Libraries and Learning." Accessed August 26, 2016.
    http://www.pewinternet.org/2016/04/07/libraries-and-learning/.

Reference and User Services Association (RUSA). 2011. "Guidelines for
    Behavioral Performance of Reference and Information Service Providers."
    Accessed August 26, 2016. http://www.ala.org/rusa/resources/guidelines/
    guidelinesbehavioral.

Ross, Celia. *Making Sense of Business Reference: A Guide for Librarians and
    Research Professionals*. Chicago, IL: ALA Editions, 2013.

Schwartz, Meredith. 2016. "Top Skills for Tomorrow's Librarians." Accessed
    August 26, 2016. http://lj.libraryjournal.com/2016/03/featured/top-skills
    -for-tomorrows-librarians-careers-2016/#_.

Shapiro, Phil. 2010. "It's Time for Public Libraries to Get Creative." Accessed
    August 26, 2016. http://www.pcworld.com/article/194960/Its_Time_for
    _Public_Libraries_to_Get_Creative.html.

Shapiro, Phil. 2010. "Public Libraries as Business Incubators." Accessed June 19, 2016. http://www.pcworld.com/article/197759/Public_Libraries_as _Business_Incubators.html.

Shumaker, David. *The Embedded Librarian: Innovative Strategies for Taking Knowledge Where It Is Needed*. Medford Township, NJ: Information Today, 2012.

Small Business Administration. 2016. "Small Business Trends." Accessed August 26, 2016. https://www.sba.gov/managing-business/running-business/energy-efficiency/sustainable-business-practices/small-business-trends.

Stengel, Geri. 2013. "Nonprofit Collaborations: Why Teaming Up Can Make Sense." Accessed August 26, 2016. http://www.forbes.com/sites/geristengel/ 2013/04/09/nonprofit-collaborations-why-teaming-up-can-make-sense/ #2b0402124c2c.

Weiss, Luise, Sophia Serlis-McPhillips, and Elizabeth Malafi. *Small Business and the Public Library: Strategies for a Successful Partnership*. Chicago, IL: ALA Editions, 2011.

Index

Alliance of Investor Education, 53
American Community Survey, 51
American FactFinder, 51
American Time Use Survey, 51
Annual Economic Surveys, 51
Arlington Heights Memorial Library
  (AHML), 84
Association of Energy Engineers, 34
AtoZ databases, 35–36

*The Basic Business Library: Core
  Resources and Services,* 60
BatchGeo, 103
*The Best Business Books Ever: The
  Most Influential Management
  Books You'll Never Have Time
  to Read,* 5
BIZLINK, 71–72
BizStats, 56
Blogger, 13
Bloomberg, 5
BNI International, 94
BPlans, 55
Branded business center card, 24
Brochures, 90–92
Brookhaven Coalition of Chambers, 78,
  80
Buffett, Jimmy, 2
Bureau of Labor Statistics, 51, 56
Business book clubs, 76
Business Books: Core Collections, 60
Business cards, 89–90
Businesses: library cards for local, 23–24;
  social media for, 73
Business Insights: Essentials, 37
Business librarian, 1–14; computer skills
  training, 10–11; do-it-yourself
  website, 12; free blog services,
  12–14; guidebook, 8; in-house
  training, 9–10; organizing informa-
  tion, 11–12; subscription database
  training, 10; wiki, 8–9
Business memberships, 24
Business networking groups, 94
Business Plans Handbook, 55
Business research, 71
Business Resource Open House, 78
Business Source Premier, 36
Business trade shows, 92–93
BusinessUSA, 56

Canva, 75
Carnegie, Dale, 5
Cherry Hill Public Library, 78
The Chief, 60
Civic associations, 94
CNBC, 5
CNN Money, 5
Cockerell, Lee, 6
Collier, Joe, 27
Comma Separated Value (CSV)
  files, 10
Competitive intelligence, 72–73
Computer skills training, 10–11
Consumer Expenditure Survey, 51
CoreLogic's RealQuest Professional, 34
Costco Warehouse Corporation, 37
Covert, Jack, 5
Covey, Stephen, 5
Coworking spaces, 32
CrunchBase, 52
*The Customer Rules: The 39 Essential
  Rules for Delivering Sensational
  Service* (Cockerell), 6

Databases: AtoZ databases, 35–36;
  Business Insights: Essentials, 37;
  Business Insights: Global, 37;
  Business Source Premier, 36;
  choosing, 34–48; D&B Million
  Dollar Database, 38–39;
  Demographics Now, 37–38;
  Foundation Directory, 39;
  LexisNexis Dossier, 40; Mergent
  Intellect, 41–42; Plunkett Research,
  42; Redbooks Library Edition, 43;
  ReferenceUSA, 44; Simmons
  OneView, 45; Small Business
  Resource Center, 46; Statista,
  47–48
DataUSA, 51
D&B Million Dollar Database, 38–39
Demographics: American FactFinder, 51;
  American Time Use Survey, 51;
  Consumer Expenditure Survey, 51;
  DataUSA, 51; Economic Census, 52;
  Pew Internet & American Life
  Project, 52
Demographics Now database, 37–38
Desk, getting away from, 27–30
Discussion groups, 76

Do-it-yourself website, 12
Downtown Kings Mountain Small
 Business Success Project, 31
Dun & Bradstreet Million Dollar
 Database, 41
Durney, Sonya, 6, 25, 26

Economic Census, 51, 52
EDGAR, 53
Embedded librarians, 30–32
Entrepreneur: becoming, 71; Entrepreneur
 Series, 70–71
Entrepreneur magazine, 4, 60
Ernsthausen, David G., 5
Etsy business, 75

Facebook, 12, 24, 66, 68, 73
Forbes, 4
Foundation Directory, 39
Fox Business, 5
Free blog services, 12–14; blogger, 13;
 Tumblr, 13; Weebly, 13–14;
 WordPress, 12–13
Freedom of Information Act (FOIA)
 request, 101
Funding: CrunchBase, 52; Grants.gov, 52

Gale Business Insights, 100
Gale/Cengage, 55, 62
GlobalEdge, 54
Google, 10, 11–12, 54
Google+, 12
Google Analytics, 21
Google Drive, 11–12, 75
Google Maps, 102–3
Grants.gov, 52
Greater Middle Country Chamber of
 Commerce, 80
Guidebook, 8
*Guidelines for Behavioral Performance of
 Reference and Information Service
 Providers,* RUSA, 8

Harvard Business Review, 60
How to Win Friends and Influence People
 (Carnegie), 5
*The 100 Best Business Books of All Time:
 What They Say, Why They Matter,
 and How They Can Help You* (Covert
 and Satterstein), 5

Illinois Library Leadership Initiative, 27
Inc. magazine, 4, 5, 60

Information, organizing, 11–12
In-house training, 9–10
Instagram, 24, 73
Investing: Investopedia, 53; Investor's
 Clearinghouse, 53; Securities and
 Exchange Commission, 53
Investopedia, 53
Investopedia Dictionary, 53
Investor's Business Daily, 60
Investor's Clearinghouse, 53

Johnson, Spencer, 5
Join.me, 75

Kittredge, Julie, 25, 84
Kmart, 37
KnowThis, 54
Kompass, 50

Lacy, Betty, 21
LexisNexis Dossier, 40
Librarians, embedded, 30–32
Library 21c, 17–18, 89
Library cards, for local businesses, 23–24
Library Journal, 25
LibraryLinkNJ, 78
LinkedIn, 24
Local businesses: library cards for, 23–24;
 one-on-one reference, 24–25; part-
 nerships, 25–27
Long Island Business News, 4
Lusitania, 3
Lyman, Jay, 25, 78, 80, 82

*Making Sense of Business Reference: A
 Guide for Librarians and Research
 Professionals* (Ross), 2, 5
Malafi, Elizabeth, 5
Manta, 51
Mapquest, 103
Marketing: GlobalEdge, 54; KnowThis,
 54; Marketing Charts, 54
Marketing Charts, 54
Market Potential Index, 54
Mauney Memorial Library, North
 Carolina, 31
McKay, Peter Z., 60
Meetup.com, 31
Mergent Intellect, 38, 41–42, 50, 99, 102,
 105
Microsoft, 10
Microsoft Excel, 10
Microsoft MapPoint, 103

Microsoft Office, 12
Microsoft Publisher, 11
Microsoft Word, 68
Middle Country Public Library, 5
Miller Business Center, 5, 60, 71, 73–74, 76, 104
Moss, Rita W., 5
Mount Prospect Entrepreneurs Initiative (MPEI), 27–28
Mount Prospect Public Library, 76

New Haven Free Public Library (NHFPL), 70
Newsday, 4
New York Public Library (NYPL), 19–21
New York State Business Services, 55
New York Times Business Day, 4
Nonprofit organizations, 95
North American Industry Classification System (NAICS), 52–53

One-on-one appointments, 24–25
One-on-one reference, 24–25
Online business reference log, 9
Open House event, 76–77

Partnerships, 25–27
Patent and Trademark Office, 54
Patent and Trademark Resource Center (PTRC), 54
Patents, 54
Patterson, James, 3
Pew Internet & American Life Project, 52
Pew Research Center, 52
Pikes Peak Library District, 17
Plunkett Research, 42
Portage District Library, 71
Portland Public Library, 25
Programming, 65–85; 3-D printing in twenty-first century, 76; apps, 75–76; art of selling yourself, 74; BIZLINK, 71–72; business book clubs/discussion groups, 76; business research essentials, 71; Business Resource Open House, 78; competitive intelligence, 72–73; entrepreneur, becoming, 71; Entrepreneur Fair, 78; Entrepreneur Series, 70–71; Etsy class, 74–75; Facebook, 73; Instagram, 73; managing social media, 73; Open House, 76–77; program ideas, 70; social media for business, 73; starting small business in Hoover, 70; strategies for generating traffic and leads at trade shows, 77; Strictly Business event, 78–85; success with an Etsy business, 75; Twitter, 73; Walk-In Wednesdays, 73–74

Real-life stories, 97–106
Redbooks Library Edition, 43
Reference and User Services Association (RUSA), 8; *Guidelines for Behavioral Performance of Reference and Information Service Providers,* 8
ReferenceUSA, 34–35, 44, 50, 98, 102–3, 104–5
RICOH, 18
Ross, Celia, 2, 5
Rotary Club, 26, 87, 93–94
RSMeans Construction Cost Data books, 62

Sanford, Heather, 31–32
Satterstein, Todd, 5
SBDC Clearinghouse, 56
SCORE, 19, 21, 26, 70–71, 78, 94. *See also* Service Corps of Retired Executives
Seat Guru, 75
Seattle Public Library (SPL), 78
Securities and Exchange Commission (SEC), 53
Service Corps of Retired Executives, 94. *See also* SCORE
The Seven Habits of Highly Successful People (Covey), 5
Shelf space: center, 16–21; corner, 16; desk, 15
Simmons OneView, 45
Slack, 75
Small Business Administration (SBA), 26, 55, 70–71, 78, 94
Small Business and the Public Library: Strategies of a Successful Partnership (Malafi), 5
Small business development agency (SBDA), 94
Small Business Development Center (SBDC), 19, 26, 70, 71, 100
Small Business Resource Center, 46
Small business support: BPlans, 55; business plans, 55; mission statements, 55; New York State Business Services, 55; SBDC

Clearinghouse, 56; Small Business Administration, 55

Snapchat, 73

Social media: for business, 73; managing, 73

Special events, 65–85; BIZLINK, 71–72; business book clubs/discussion groups, 76; Business Resource Open House, 78; Entrepreneur Fair, 78; Open House, 76–77; Strictly Business event, 78–85; Walk-In Wednesdays, 73–74

Stack, Sharon, 31–32

Standard Industry Classification (SIC) code, 53, 100

Starbucks, 98

Statista database, 47–48

Statistics: BizStats, 56; Bureau of Labor Statistics, 56; BusinessUSA, 56; ZanRan numerical data search, 56–57

Strauss's Handbook of Business Information: A Guide for Librarians, Students and Researchers (Moss and Ernsthausen), 5

Strictly Business event, 78–85; basic timeline for, 83–84; Strictly Business flyer, 79; typical floor plan for, 81

Subscription database training, 10

Supreme Court Reporter, 61

Target, 37

Technology and Entrepreneurship Talent Network of New Jersey, 78

ThomasNet, 53, 104. *See also* Thomas Register of American Manufacturers

Thomas Register of American Manufacturers, 53. *See also* ThomasNet

Thomson Reuters, 61

Thornton, Bryce, 6

3-D printing in twenty-first century, 76

Trademarks, 54

Trader Joe's, 105

Trade shows, 77

Tumblr, 13

Tunity, 75

Twitter, 24, 73

USA Today, 4

U.S. Census, 38, 51, 52

U.S. Department of Agriculture: National Farmer's Market Directory, 104

U.S. Patent Office, 54

Virtual services, 21–22

Walk-In Wednesdays event, 73–74

Wall Street Journal, 4, 16, 60, 76

WalMart, 37

Weebly, 13–14

Whole Foods, 105

Who Moved My Cheese? (Johnson), 5, 76

Wiki, 8–9

Woodworth, Andy, 66–67, 78

WordPress, 12–13, 22

World War I, 3

Yahoo Maps, 103

YouTube, 10

ZanRan, 56

Zarsky, Terry, 19, 88–89

About the Authors

SALVATORE DiVINCENZO is the librarian at Middle Country Public Library in Centereach, New York. He served as the chairperson of the Reference and User Services Association/Business Reference and Services Section's (RUSA/BRASS) Business Reference in Public Libraries Committee of the American Library Association (ALA) and was the recipient of the Morningstar Public Librarian Support Award in 2013. His career experience before entering the library world includes working for a digital advertising agency, providing high-level technical support for a software company, and international sales. DiVincenzo holds a bachelor's degree in business administration from Dowling College in Oakdale, New York, and a master's degree in library science from Clarion University of Pennsylvania.

ELIZABETH MALAFI is coordinator of the Miller Business Center at the Middle Country Public Library in Centereach, New York. She is coauthor of *Small Business and the Public Library*, a guide for librarians to connect with their business communities. In 2014, she was part of the team that developed *Financial Literacy Education in Libraries: Guidelines and Best Practices for Service* for ALA. Malafi is active in the business librarian community, having served as member-at-large for the Executive Committee of BRASS and as chair of BRASS's Business Reference in Public Libraries Committee. In 2008, she was awarded the D&B Public Librarian Support Award. In 2017, Malafi was awarded the prestigious BRASS Mergent by FTSE Russell Excellence in Business Librarianship Award. Prior to becoming a librarian, she worked in the sales departments of several publishing houses.